moulding
assembling
designing

Ceramics in Architecture

contents

A conversation with David Baena, Toni Gironès and Vicente Sarrablo

This introduction is based on an extract from a conversation held between three architects who are extremely familiar with ceramics, both as a traditional and novel material. The questions, which refer to projects described in this book, served as a basis for a spontaneous dialogue which dealt with clearly relevant themes such as the relationship between designers and this material, the potential for innovation and the relations with manufacturers.

How can architects be encouraged to use ceramics?

DB The ceramic tile is culturally very close to us. It has always been here, it's a material that speaks for itself; its textures, colours and shapes are qualities easily perceived by the user. For architects, it's now a basic material that can be used to create images, surfaces and volumes which go beyond the traditional view of the material.

VS I always advise my students that when they are going to introduce an innovation into a project for a client, it is easier to do so with a familiar material. Ceramic meets this condition and easily fires the clients' enthusiasm, even if it comes in a completely novel format. And nowadays, there are good examples of innovative architecture where ceramics plays a lead role.

In your opinion, to what extent does this extraordinarily familiar material lend itself to innovation and creativity?

TG If, by innovation we are referring to originality in the sense of a formal artifice or device, then we are providing superficial and incomplete solutions. Unfortunately, originality doesn't always draw on its origins, by this I mean, treating and working with a material using common sense. I think it would be worth trying to free modern-day society of certain prejudices. Previously, the wear on the material was part of the project. Now it seems everything has to be flawless, frozen in time, which is a contradiction because the material cannot be dis-associated from the passing of time. In this respect I consider it our job to change certain specific attitudes. First ours and then the clients'.

Architects should not be obsessed with planning and inventing what
has already been invented, because, often, simply by looking or taking
a different approach, things turn out to already exist; it's just a
question of giving them a new application or a change of direction.
It is true that sometimes one can speak of prototypes and new pieces,
but there's no doubt that they have their roots in basic pre-existing
concepts, which have simply been reinterpreted. Obviously we live in
a time of enormous technological progress, and high technology can be
profitably applied to ceramic without losing sight of the intrinsic
nature of the material.

VS Where there are still big surprises in store is in the use of
ceramics on exteriors. In Japan, I was really surprised by the fact
that the majority of the tall buildings are completely covered by
ceramics, using a system I've never seen used in Europe. It consists
of concrete panels which, instead of being painted, incorporate pieces
of stoneware as part of their finish. During their manufacture, the
stoneware pieces are laid face down so that the biscuit is face up at
the bottom of the mould. The backs of the tiles are dovetailed to
improve their adherence to the concrete which is poured over them.
When it has set, they remove the shuttering leaving the tiles
incrusted in the oncrete. It's impressive that over half the buildings
in Tokyo are clad with these panels and they still look fine after
years have gone by.

moulding   **What conclusions can be drawn on weighing up the formal possibilities
and the technical limitations of ceramics? Would you say that it still
has potential for development?**

DB There's no doubt that the arrival of large formats has represented
a qualitative and quantitative change in the use of ceramics,
especially in the case of wall coverings and claddings, but I think
it is even more important to retrieve the three-dimensional aspect of
the material. Although it is initially a plastic mouldable material,
we generally view ceramic as a laminate. Laminates make up 95% of
the products on the market. Research should now be carried out into
the textures and the relief of the pieces, not so much with the idea
of joining pieces together to form three dimensional structures,
but rather so that the pieces themselves present textures on the
basis of the moulding process. The industry should be able to
produce forms and mouldings with elements and ceramic pieces in
three dimensions. The ability to create textures would benefit the
image of ceramics.

VS Before, when you ordered special pieces, depending on what manufacturer you went to, formats greater than 40 cm were complicated
to produce because the presses, the conveyor belts or the trays which
went into the kilns were not designed for materials in large formats.
But now in this country, they have begun to produce pieces which
measure up to 1.20 m. It's a real challenge for the manufacturers.

DB Until a few years ago, the pending issue in ceramics manufacture was
to get past small and medium-size formats. At last they've managing
to find ways of working with large formats.

VS   I've seen single sheets of extruded ceramic which measure 1.80 m in
     length. There is still a need to develop technologies which can be
     applied to the manufacture of such large formats. Because to cover a
     window opening measuring 1 m or 1.20 m, you need two or three pieces
     measuring 40 o 50 cm, but if you cover the whole opening with a single
     piece of the same dimensions, it's much easier. Another recent inven-
     tion is a piece just 3 mm thick with a surface area of 3 x 1 m. With
     this ceramic piece, you can clad surfaces as if you were using MDF or
     metal plate. And three metres is enough to reach from floor to ceiling.
     Nonetheless, the arrival of large formats doesn't necessarily mean that
     traditional techniques are being lost. Take the case of the enormous
     pieces which Paredes&Pedrosa used for the Auditorium in Peñíscola.

designing   **Could you explain where your interests in ceramics lie as architects?**
                 What roused your interest in developing design proposals using this
                 material?

VS   There are buildings covered with ceramics which are many years old and
     still look the same as when they were built. They are impeccable.

DB   Although it doesn't look as if time has gone by, in fact time doesn't
     pass in vain. What happens is that the material ages well, nobly.
     A stroll next to old brick walls, maybe centuries old, gives me a
     feeling of tranquillity, of silence, of the reliability of the
     material — there are really very few materials which are dignified
     by the passing of time.

TG   What I find more interesting is not so much that the materials should
     look as if they were still brand-new, which I find a bit odd, but that
     they age well. This denotes the fineness of the material.

VS   Something which isn't generally realised about ceramics, and I think
     it's one of the most interesting points, is that there is a wide range
     of products with different porosity and, therefore, different ageing
     characteristics. Porcelain tiles behave almost like glass and they
     have the practically the same mechanical characteristics. When large-
     format porcelain tiles are fixed to a façade, it's as if the façade
     was clad with glass. For this reason the passing of time is not so
     perceptible because it has practically no porosity. We need to learn
     about all the possibilities of ceramics, from the most porous, tradi-
     tional, handmade, artisanal pieces, with better or worse joints
     — because ageing is also noticeable in the joints between the pieces —
     to pieces that are unaffected by ageing because, like glass, they are
     resistant to it.

TG   One thing that interests me about ceramics is that it shouldn't need
     any maintenance. The Japanese don't clean silver or bronze; they just
     let it film over and leave it as it is. Ceramic doesn't require main-
     tenance. That is, it's a porous material which evolves through time.

assembling   **The manufacturers offer mass-produced pieces, which brings us to the**
                 idea of assembling, the physical union of the pieces. Do you think
                 this idea of assembling should be linked to a re-evaluation of the
                 existing systems for the application of ceramics in projects?

DB   Ceramics have the same magic as Lego: starting with module, a
     universal piece, it's possible to arrive at a large number of diffe-
     rent structures. There are few materials which have this capacity for
     combination. With a single piece, it's possible to create an incalcu-
     lable number of forms absolutely distinct from each other.

VS   I strongly encourage my students to try and design reusable pieces,
     so that other architects can play with them.

DB   Like that, the design is open to modification and someone else can
     reinterpret it.

TG   In this respect it's a question of projecting a system of pieces based
     on very simple forms. Sometimes, somebody invents a game with of
     pieces, while others project systems.

**What do you think would be the best way to encourage manufacturers to
undertake new projects? How do you think personalised requirements can
be reconciled with the need for standardisation?**

DB   I think there are sufficient examples of where the industry has suc-
     cessfully developed a product and manufacture has gone ahead. So we
     can rest assured that the new generation of ceramic products will find
     a good market, provided that the qualities of the materials are fully
     valued and exploited and lines of technical and formal research in
     conjunction with professional designers are encouraged.

TG   Ceramics have specific properties. As architects we can persuade a
     manufacturer to develop a piece which can be produced in different
     versions. What is interesting is to design a piece that can later
     generate different functional interpretations.

VS   In the ceramics faculty, we try to encourage cooperation between manu-
     facturers and architects, because we architects are often very poorly
     informed about the production costs of a piece and are unfamiliar with
     the production processes. We try to draw a balance between the two
     worlds, the one which tends towards standardisation and must keep an
     eye on the business side, and the other which towards personalisation
     and the search for innovation. I've found manufacturers willing to
     make considerable efforts to understand the thinking of architects and
     work together with them. And when this cooperation is mutual, the
     results are surprising. It's quite wonderful.

Many thanks to David Baena, Toni Gironès and Vicente Sarrablo
Barcelona, November 2005

House in Cascais
Portugal

When designing a house, the problem is to understand the character of both the client and the site in order to invent an "alter ego". Our capacity for repetition depends on our attitude at the "time" and on the personality of the "place". Thus, I became interested in doors and windows, which I had had inhibitions about for 25 years.

A vast horizontal expanse of sea, the Atlantic, cannot be recorded: an ocean — always different, always the same — cannot be "captured". We therefore opened up a neutral view, expanding the openings and designing with positive and negative volumes. The materials and colours are all different, all the same: grey. The grey tones vary gradually from the outside to the inside. The greys of the Azulino de Cascais stone, the matt sheen of the aluminium and the sand-blasted stainless steel all await the blaze of the setting sun to lift them out of their "grey" state.

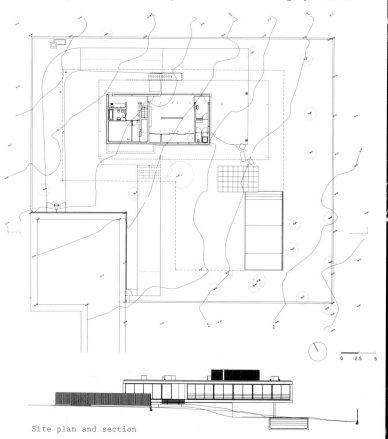

0   2.5   5

Site plan and section

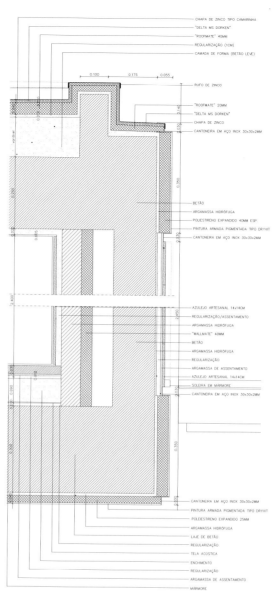

CHAPA DE ZINCO TIPO CAMARINHA
"DELTA MS DORKEN"
"ROOFMATE" 40MM
REGULARIZAÇÃO (1CM)
CAMADA DE FORMA (BETÃO LEVE)

0.100   0.175   0.055

RUFO DE ZINCO

"ROOFMATE" 20MM
"DELTA MS DORKEN"
CHAPA DE ZINCO
CANTONEIRA EM AÇO INOX 30x30x2MM

BETÃO
ARGAMASSA HIDRÓFUGA
POLIESTIRENO EXPANDIDO 40MM ESP.
PINTURA ARMADA PIGMENTADA TIPO DRYVIT
CANTONEIRA EM AÇO INOX 30x30x2MM

AZULEJO ARTESANAL 14x14CM
REGULARIZAÇÃO/ASSENTAMENTO
ARGAMASSA HIDRÓFUGA
"WALLMATE" 40MM
BETÃO
ARGAMASSA HIDRÓFUGA
REGULARIZAÇÃO
ARGAMASSA DE ASSENTAMENTO
AZULEJO ARTESANAL 14x14CM
SOLEIRA EM MÁRMORE
CANTONEIRA EM AÇO INOX 30x30x2MM

CANTONEIRA EM AÇO INOX 30x30x2MM
PINTURA ARMADA PIGMENTADA TIPO DRYVIT
POLIESTIRENO EXPANDIDO 25MM
ARGAMASSA HIDRÓFUGA
LAJE DE BETÃO
REGULARIZAÇÃO
TELA ACÚSTICA
ENCHIMENTO
REGULARIZAÇÃO
ARGAMASSA DE ASSENTAMENTO
MÁRMORE

North façade section (kitchen)

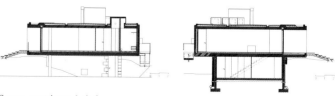

Cross sections 1 + 2

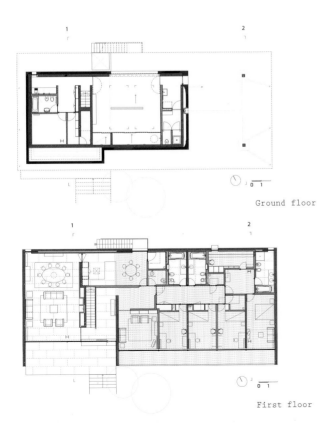

Ground floor

First floor

ARCHITECT: Eduardo Souto de Moura LOCATION: Praceta dos Ameeiros, Lote nº 2, Cascais, Portugal DESIGN: 1994 CONSTRUCTION: 2002 DESIGN TEAM: Eduardo Souto de Moura with Nuno Graça Moura, Camilo Rebelo, José Carlos Mariano CLIENT: Luís Valadas Fernandes CONTRACTOR: Promafer STRUCTURAL ENGINEER: Adão da Fonseca & Associados ELECTRICAL ENGINEER: Rodrigues Gomes & Associados MECHANICAL ENGINEER: Rodrigues Gomes & Associados PHOTOGRAPHER: Luís Ferreira Alves

TILE: glazed wall tiles
DIMENSIONS: 10 x 10 cm

The Atelier Luc Peire Complex: Jenny and Luc Peire Foundation
Knokke, Belgium

Few Flemish artists have lived in so many different places and had as many workshops as Luc Peire (1916-1994). This leading representative of abstract verticalism in Europe changed abode regularly, producing a coherent oeuvre with single-minded determination from no less than 26 locations. One address, however, remained his "home port" throughout. This was his atelier in Knokke's De Judestraat, behind the "Villa Lucia".

The project in the De Judestraat in Knokke had three parts. First and foremost, restoring the atelier to its original condition, to enable the visitor to experience the atmosphere and intimacy of Luc Peire's work-space. The renovation work for the atelier consisted of a structural consolidation without changing the character of the space or its furnishings. The largest and most visible addition is the new building on the street side, which contains the exhibition space and a large area for storing the works bequeathed to the Foundation after Peire's death.

To make way for the new building, the house on the street side was bought back by the Foundation in 1997 and demolished in 2000. The site itself is 8.50 metres wide and 49 metres deep.

For the outer façade, the architects chose a severe composition with squares as the basic element. Just as Peire composed his canvases with extreme precision, so too the architects sought precise command of the outer face of the new building. As their material they chose tiles with a special 20 x 20 cm format. The slight change in format and the different shades of grey-blue colouring produce an at-once severe and surprisingly chequered expression.

The solidity of the façade is softened by running the glazed surface right up to the edge of the roof. The fine detail work stands out, with brass profiles used both for the frames and to form the transition between the darker tiles and the white Thassos marble tablet in which the name of the Jenny and Luc Peire Foundation is discreetly inscribed.

For the entrance, the architects opted for a small recess, all in white in contrast to the dark tiles. The passage between the street and the garden of the original lay-out was maintained, a functional element combined with the memory of the location. This corridor can serve to exhibit smaller works, like Peire's graphic works or sketches, or small sculptures by artists in a similar style.

Flanking this corridor is a second and larger exhibition area, with blank walls on three sides on which works can be placed. This upward striving space is the dominant theme of the Foundation's 7.50-metre, two-storey-high entrance foyer. The exhibition area receives direct daylight from the single outside window. The closed side wall reinforces the sense of length of the plot and the view from the interior out onto the garden. The rear façade of the main volume is covered with the same dark tiles as the street side, whilst the extension is cement-faced with a colourless protective coating.

The outcome is a building quietly and unfussily positioned in this residential street.

STICHTING·FONDATION
JENNY EN LUC PEIRE

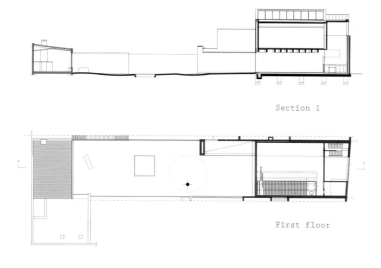

Section 1

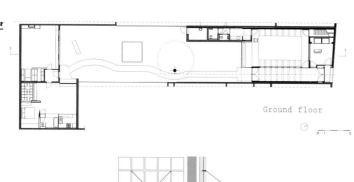

First floor

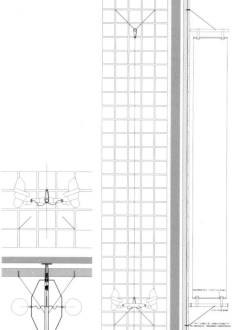

Ground floor

0 1 5

Façade details

ARCHITECTS: Peter De Bruycker, Inge De Brock
LOCATION: De Judestraat 64, 8300 Knokke, Belgium
DESIGN: 1999 **CONSTRUCTION:** 2002-2003 **CLIENT:** Jenny and
Luc Peire Foundation **CONTRACTOR:** Neirynck& Zn, 9990
Maldegem **STRUCTURAL ENGINEER:** VK Engineering, 8200
Brugge **TEXT:** Marc Dubois

TILE: glazed stoneware tiles
DIMENSIONS: 20 x 20 cm

Surgery
Castellar del Vallès, Spain

The site is located at one end of a block reserved for public facilities, within a recent urban development. Another public building of the same size was to be built at the other end of the block, while the space in-between was destined to become a public garden.

The building spreads and occupies the site as far as the building codes permit. Thus, an enclosure of 45 x 26.5 metres is obtained, which will contain the entire programme of the building.

The entire site is filled, although in two different manners: the surgery areas — the largest and most important part of the brief — extend across the ground like a thick heavy carpet with holes regularly punched out to allow light and air to penetrate. All other public areas are concentrated at the other end of the site. The entrance hall — a through way that joins the street and the future public garden — simultaneously unites and separates the two parts. The staff areas are located on the upper floor.

The surgery areas are built by applying a system of aggregation that begins with what was identified, through a new approach to the programme, as the minimal functional unit: a doctor's surgery, a nurse's surgery and a waiting room. A patio accompanies each waiting room, supplying natural light and a recognisable identity. Each pair of these functional units forms a larger unit — general medicine, paediatrics, etc. — which can be identified through the colour of one of its patios. Thus each of the patios becomes unique and recognisable and — through its dimensions, position in plan and texture — part of a series.

Narrower, longitudinal patios are placed along the axis of the building in order to provide natural light and ventilation to those surgeries that are not placed along the building's perimeter.

A continuous skin of brick wraps the building, responding, through its texture, to the varying requirements for light, ventilation and privacy.

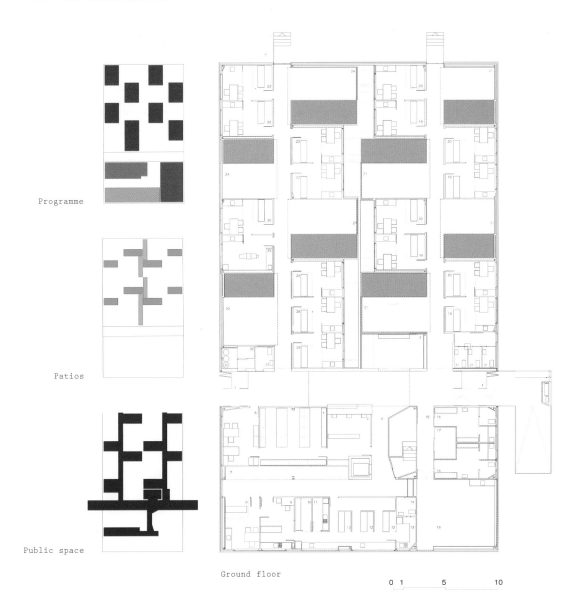

Programme

Patios

Public space

Ground floor

0 1   5   10

ARCHITECTS: Charmaine Lay, Carles Muro, Quim Rosell
LOCATION: Castellar del Vallès, Spain **DESIGN:** 1995
(competition) **CONSTRUCTION:** 1998-99 **DESIGN TEAM:**
Charmaine Lay, Carles Muro and Quim Rosell with
Lluís Ortega **QUANTITY SURVEYOR:** Anna Moreno **CONSTRUCTION
SURVEYOR:** Josep Vila (Taller d'Enginyeries) **CLIENT:**
Servei Català de la Salut **CONTRACTOR:** CORSAN **STRUCTURAL
ENGINEER:** Gerardo Rodríguez (STATIC) **SERVICES ENGINEER:**
Albert Salazar (Instal·lacions Arquitectòniques)
PHOTOGRAPHERS: Jordi Bernadó (p16-17 down and
up left, p18), Eva Serrats (p17 up right)

COURTYARD TILE: ceramic wall tiles
DIMENSIONS: 10 x 20 cm
ENTRANCE HALL, STAIRCASE AND PARTS OF THE WAITING ROOMS TILE:
porcelain tiles
DIMENSIONS: 5 x 5 cm

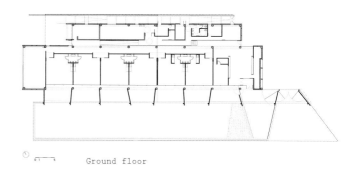

Ground floor

Infant Primary School Building
Polinyà, Spain

In dealing with a building measuring approximately 1000 m^2 to be built in 5 months, a system of wholly precast reinforced concrete columns, beams, slabs and façade panels was employed. To avoid the excessively hard appearance of such industrialised buildings, we clad with coloured tiles separating screen walls in an open arcade sheltering outdoor classroom areas. In this way, and with careful attention to the section, the harshness of the volume is softened. And the school children can recognise their classrooms by bright colours that are reflected on the timber ceiling of the arcade, the entire area being impregnated with a very special light.

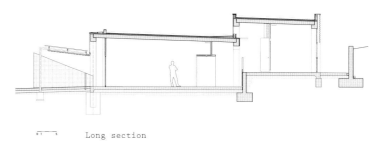

Long section

Site plan

ARCHITECTS: Vicente Sarrablo, Cristina Castelao, Jordi Roviras, Héctor Jala **LOCATION:** Polinyà, Spain **COMPLETION:** September 2004 **CLIENT:** Gestió d'Infrastructures, S.A. **CONTRACTOR:** Bosch Pascual Construcciones **STRUCTURAL ENGINEER:** Juan Ignacio Eskubi **SITE MANAGER:** Àlex Martín i Torralba **SITE SUPERINTENDENT:** Juan Cerezo

TILE: glazed stoneware tiling
DIMENSIONS: 10 x 10 cm

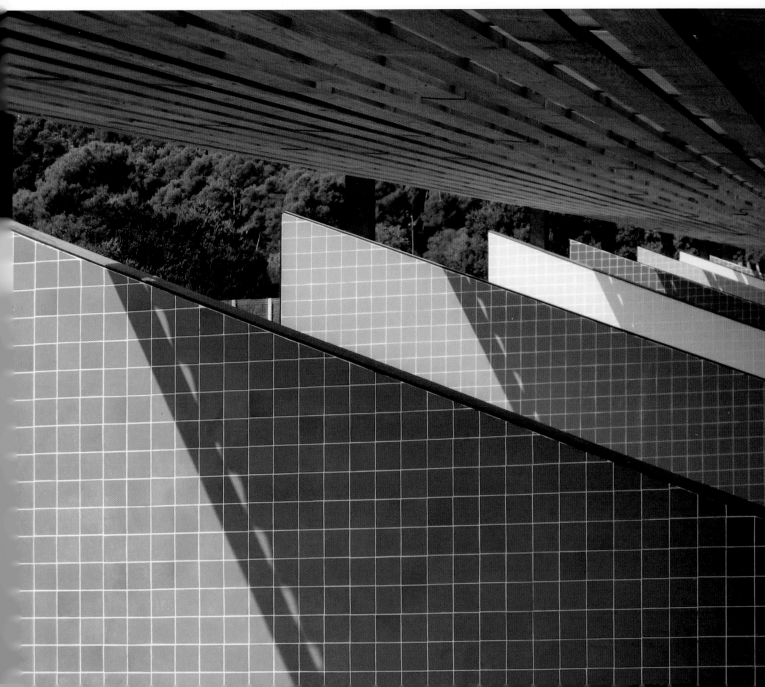

Portuguese Pavilion, Expo 2000
Hanover, Germany

The Portuguese pavilion for the Hanover Fair was a prefabricated and portable building, designed for later installation in Portugal. The volume, a parallelepiped, keeps to the outline of the site at a distance of five metres from the boundaries. The structure consists of prefabricated steel beams and pillars, covered with exterior panelling and varnished black conglomerate cork blocks. The building is square in shape, but one wing extends as far as the street. The dihedron formed by the façades of these two volumes delineates an open courtyard, covered with glazed tiles.

The building is distributed on two floors, both used as exhibition space. The first floor was designated the VIP area, with a small auditorium and the administration services. The part of the building that extends as far as the street was faced with limestone and bears the word Portugal in letters in low relief. The surrounding strips of ground were gravelled over.

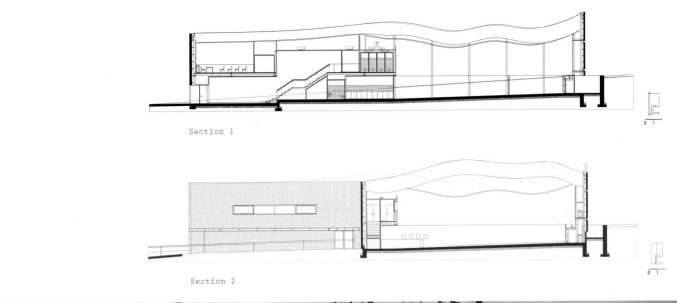

Section 1

Section 2

0.500
0.177 0.173 0.150

8.000 ▽
COPPER FLASHING ▽

7.600 ▽

7.200 ▽
CORK (2cm)
CH 5mm

SHS 100

0.300
0.150

"VIÚVA LAMEGO " TILES, 14x14cm (GLUED)
BLACK CONGLOMERATE CORK BLOCKS 20x15x100CM
VIROC BOARD (COMP SED WOOD/CEMENT)
WATERPROOFING PAINT
ROCKWOOL
STRUCTURAL SUPPORT (CV75)
PLASTER BOARD "KNAUF" (2x12,5mm)

HEB 400

STEEL PLATE (5mm) OVER AUDITORIUM DOOR

5.302
CH 10mm
STEEL FRAME "JANSEN"

1.187

VARIABLE HEIGHT (MINIMUM 3.840)

1.100

AUDITORIUM

4.165   2%

0.885

1.000

ROCKWOOL
STRUCTURAL SUPPORT (CV75)
PLASTER BOARD "KNAUF" (2x12,5mm)
PAINTED CORK (5mm)
PAINTED STEEL BAR (60x5mm)

3.280 ▽
3.185 (ROHBAU) ▽

HEA 160

0.500

2.840 ▽
2.760 ▽

PLASTER BOARD "KNAUF" (2x12,5mm)
STRUCTURAL SUPPORT (CV50)

LOWER CEILING ACCORDING TO LIGHT PROJECT

CORK (6mm)
VIROC BOARD (19mm)
BLACK CORK CONGLOMERATE (20mm)
VIROC BOARD (28mm)
PLASTIC MEMBRANE
"TRAPEZBLECH" ("HOESCH" E85 t=0.088)
ROCK-WOOL
STRUCTURAL SUPPORT (CV50)
PLASTER BOARD "KNAUF" (2x12,5mm)

ROCKWOOL
STRUCTURAL SUPPORT (CV75)
PLASTER BOARD "KNAUF" (2x12,5mm)

3.180

VIP HALL

"VIÚVA LAMEGO " TILES, 14x14cm (GLUED)
BLACK CONGLOMERATE CORK BLOCKS 20x15x100CM
VIROC BOARD (COMPOSED WOOD/CEMENT)
WATERPROOFING PAINT

GRAVEL

PAINTED STEELPLATE (150x5mm)

INSULATION 6CM (CORK)
CONCRETE WALL
WATERPROOFING MEMBRANE
DRAINING MEMBRANE

0.420 ▽
0.520 ▽

0.150 0.350 0.340

S20.06

0   1

Façade section

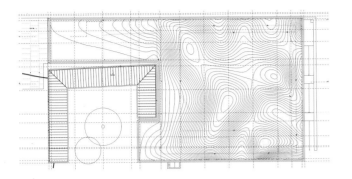

Roof plan

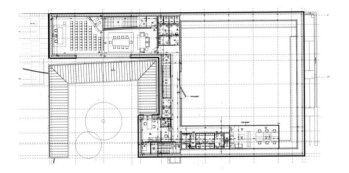

First floor

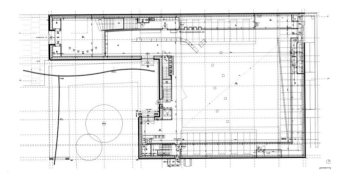

Ground floor

ARCHITECTS: Álvaro Siza and Eduardo Souto de Moura
LOCATION: Expo 2000 Hanover, Germany **DESIGN:** 1999
CONSTRUCTION: 1999-2000 **DESIGN TEAM:** Álvaro Siza Vieira and
Eduardo Souto de Moura with Nuno Graça Moura, Ricardo
Rosa Santos, Carlo Nozza, José Carlos Mariano, Jorge
Domingues **CLIENT:** Portugal 2001, S.A **MAIN CONTRACTOR:**
Philipp Holzmann A.G., Empreiteiros Casais, S.A.
STRUCTURAL ENGINEER: Ove Arup & Partners, Adão da Fonseca
& Associados **SERVICES ENGINEER:** Ove Arup & Partners,
Adão da Fonseca & Associados **MECHANICAL ENGINEER:** Ove
Arup & Partners, Adão da Fonseca & Associados **ACOUSTIC**
CONSULTANT: Ove Arup & Partners, Adão da Fonseca &
Associados **PHOTOGRAPHER:** Christian Richters

TILE: glazed wall tile
DIMENSIONS: 14 x 14 cm

Ceramic Showroom
Graz, Austria

The purpose of this new building is to house a ceramic showroom and storage facilities. The narrow site, surrounded by heavy traffic, suggested a compact building able to accommodate the comparatively demanding need for usable space. It was very clear from the outset that ceramic tiles would play an integral part in the design, both inside and outside the building, as they would be a logical symbol for the products on show.

The external wall consists of an alternating concrete system with elements partly cast in-situ and partly prefabricated. The undulating façade is divided into strips by small square blocks which create horizontal openings through which light and air can circulate in and out of the building. The exterior surfaces of the undulating walls are clad in glass mosaic — the most appropriate covering for curved surfaces. The mosaic combines three different shades of orange and was specially commissioned for this project. The shine of the material sets off the expressive plasticity of the four identical façades. The prefabricated concrete elements inside the building have an attractive finish and combine with the other parts of the building to provide a complete concrete backdrop that shows off the ceramic tiles at their best.

Section

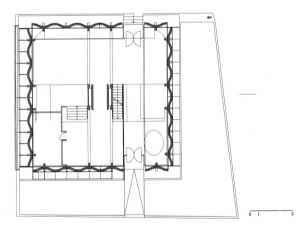

Ground floor

0 1 5

ARCHITECTS: Leeb Condak Architekten **LOCATION:** Puchstrasse 20, Graz, Austria **DESIGN:** 1998 **CONSTRUCTION:** 1998-1999 **CLIENT:** Fliesen Leeb **STRUCTURAL ENGINEER:** Engelbert Lutz **SERVICES ENGINEER:** Alois Schuster **CONTRACTOR:** Strobl Bau, Weiz **PHOTOGRAPHERS:** Paul Ott (p27), Peter Leeb (p26)

TILE: glass mosaic
DIMENSIONS: 2 x 2 cm

Award-winner in the 1st Edition of Tile of Spain Awards of Architecture and Interior Design (2002-2003)

Ceramic tiles: production process, types and fixing techniques

Ceramic tiles include glazed wall tiles, paving tiles and roofing tiles, and are thin slabs used to cover, by definition, walls, floors and roofs.

Traditionally, ceramic tiles were made with earth, water, air and fire. And this is still the case.
They are made with mineral substances, mainly clay, finely broken up and compressed. To give them the right shape, a certain amount of moisture is necessary, i.e., water, but once the pieces have been moulded, they must be dried out, and air is needed for this. Many pieces are given a vitreous mineral glaze on the facing surface.
And lastly, the pieces acquire their characteristic hardness thanks to the firing process. The undersides of the pieces have bumps or ribs whose purpose is to help the pieces adhere to the support surface.

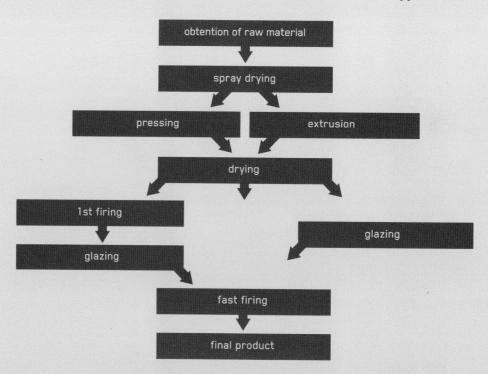

TYPES OF CERAMIC TILES

The absorption of water in relation to the mass of the tile (as a measure of porosity) and the moulding technique are two criteria used to classify ceramic tiles in accordance with international ISO and European EN standards.

Water absorption is considered very low if it is under 0.5% (Group Ia); low if it is under 3% (Group Ib); medium up to 10% (Group II); and high if it is over 10% (Group III). The absorption of water has a bearing on some important characteristics of ceramic tiles, in particular their mechanical strength and frost-resistance. The most commonly used moulding techniques are extrusion (Group A) and dry-pressing (Group B). The moulding technique depends on certain specifications, particularly the dimensions of the pieces. Lastly, the tiles may be unglazed (UGL) or glazed (GL). The type of glaze determines the tile's resistance to abrasion. All the ceramic tiles currently manufactured in Spain in significant quantities can be classified within these categories.

Extruded Ceramic Tiles Clay is mixed with enough water to obtain a plastic paste which is moulded by forcing it under pressure through a series of nozzles in a machine known as an extruding press. The resulting continuous line of pressed clay is then cut into pieces of the desired length.

1 Extruded ceramic tiles

1

The pieces made using this moulding method have a characteristic finish on the underside, consisting of parallel ribs or grooves. On the base or underside of these tiles, small imperfections (pores, inclusions) can be observed, and also on the top side and the edges. This makes them very suitable for rustic constructions or simply to achieve an intentional rustic effect. The majority of extruded ceramic tiles are unglazed and single fired.

The Spanish output of extruded ceramic tiles is some 20 million square metres, equivalent to 3% of total production. Three types are in steady production:

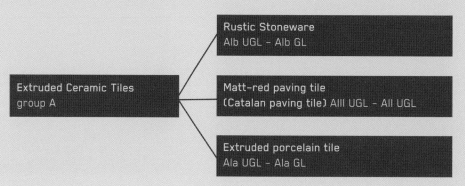

Rustic stoneware tiles have low water absorption and a dark brown base; a small amount are glazed or given a superficial treatment (salt-glazed stoneware) which makes them suitable for façades. They are used as interior flooring in rustic settings and industrial buildings, but more often as exterior paving for public spaces.

Matt red paving tiles or Catalan paving tiles, with high or medium-high water absorption, have a reddish base and are used in temperate climates for terraces and balconies, more usually in country residences.

Extruded porcelain tile, with very low water absorption, has characteristics and uses analogous to dry-pressed porcelain tiles. It may be glazed or unglazed. Moulding by extrusion allows the manufacture of specialty tiles, such as the pieces needed for swimming pools (overflows, drainage channels and so on). It is a new product, developed in Spain. Its use is gradually increasing.

Dry-pressed Ceramic Tiles The pieces are moulded from a mix of clays ground down to a fine powder. One method is to dry and grind the clay in hammer or pendulum mills to obtain an impalpable powder. For purposes of moulding, the clay is given plasticity by adding a small proportion of water.

A more modern technique, generalised in Spain, is wet-grinding: the clay, with plenty of water and siliceous balls, is loaded into a batch ball mill, which consists of a hollow steel cylinder lined with rubber or inert mineral compounds. The rotation of the mill produces a aqueous suspension of clay, which is then sprayed into large driers or atomisers, where the water is evaporated by a stream of hot air. This produces minute granules of powdered clay, spherical in shape, which retain sufficient moisture to give them plasticity. The powder or granules are moulded in high-pressure presses to produces pieces of the desired shape and dimensions. Those pieces which will not be glazed are single fired, and this concludes the production process.

The great majority of dry-pressed ceramic tiles are glazed. To glaze the tiles, a watery suspension of glaze made from minerals, mainly silica, colourings and fluxes is applied to the surface of the tile. This is vitrified by firing and adheres inseparably to the tile. The oldest process consists of double firing. First the tiles are fired to obtain the body or base, and then the glaze is applied and vitrified in a second firing.

The single firing technique consists of applying glaze to the unfired tiles and single firing them. This method is used almost universally in Spanish production. The diamond-tips or ribs on the underside of the pressed pieces are not distributed in any particular direction. They may be square, hexagonal, round like buttons and so on. The faces and edges of the pieces are even and clear-cut, except when they are designed to look rustic. The base is fine-textured, especially if the clay was wet-milled. Dry-pressed ceramic tiles are those produced in greater quantity and variety, in three groups: wall tiles, glazed stoneware and porcelain tiles.

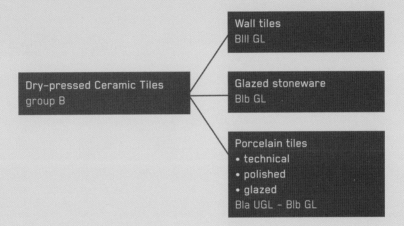

Dry-pressed Ceramic Tiles
group B

Wall tiles
BIII GL

Glazed stoneware
BIb GL

Porcelain tiles
• technical
• polished
• glazed
BIa UGL – BIb GL

Wall tiles are dry-pressed, glazed pieces with water absorption over 10%, so they are not suitable for outside use except in temperate climates. In general, the glaze shows low resistance to abrasion. Therefore, they are used predominantly for interior walls. They make up 39% of Spanish production, around 250 million square metres of tiles per annum. They are manufactured in a great range of colours, with a smooth, gloss or satin finish, marbled, veined and decorated. The exposed face is usually smooth, but may have some relief in the

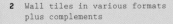
2 Wall tiles in various formats plus complements

2

form of *martelés* and bevelled edges or perimeter lines. Their usual
size is between 10 x 10 cm and 45 x 60 cm or even larger.
<u>Glazed stoneware</u> has low water absorption and is generally manufac-
tured with abrasion-resistant glazes. It is used preferably for paving
interior floors, but is also suitable for walls and outside floors
where there is no risk of extremely low temperatures. In the case of
outside floors it is best to use tiles with a good grip and good
resistance to abrasion. They make up 46% of production in Spain,

3 and 4 Glazed stoneware floor
tiles

3

4

around 300 million square metres of tiles per annum. There is an
enormous range: tiles may come in plain colours, veined, decorated
with different patterns or with finishes that imitate ornamental
stone or mosaic; they may be gloss, satin, or matt, or rustic and have
an uneven surface or a surface with relief or non-slip treatments.
The usual dimensions range from 10 x 10 cm to 60 x 60 cm and although
the predominant shape is rectangular, there are also pieces with
chamfered corners or in other polygonal formats.
<u>Porcelain tile</u> is the product with the lowest water absorption, less
than 0.5% of its own mass, which makes it suitable for exterior use
including regions affected by freezing temperatures. Although
this is the newest product in the range, introduced little more than
a decade ago (while wall tiles have been used since ancient times),
several varieties have been created in succession. The original porcelain tile is unglazed and the colour it takes on is the result of the
addition of inorganic colouring agents to the clay. Initially, it was
marketed in the same state as it came out of the kiln, with a matt
finish (technical porcelain) suitable for paving interiors and exte-

5 Porcelain tiles

5

riors, including industrial premises. Shortly after, production was diversified and polished porcelain began to appear on the market. It is obtained by polishing the exposed face of the tiles with a mechanical burnisher; this can be used for interior walls and façades.

More recently, the production of glazed porcelain tiles started with no requirement of colouring agent added previously to the body or base of the tiles. Its use is similar to glazed stoneware, but its low water ab-sorption makes it ideal for places exposed to extremely low temperatures.

6   7

Diversification and Finishes Apart from the basic range, all these types of tile include a series of complementary pieces (mouldings, listels, friezes, trims, etc.) and special ones with functional purposes (skirting, weathering, etc.). There are also sets of pieces for specific purposes (steps, risers and stringers for staircases; overflows and drainage channels for swimming pools; etc.) and ranges of sizes in modules (for example, 40 x 40 cm, 40 x 20 cm, 40 x 10 cm, 10 x 10 cm). Lastly, there is mosaic, made up of small pieces. Laying is facilitated by fixing them on a backing of paper or cloth, and this conserves the layout and the desired distances.

Ceramic tiles, once the manufacturing process is completed, can be treated with different finishes. The technique of polishing the tile's surface, mentioned previously with regard to porcelain tiles, is also applied to a small proportion of glazed paving tiles and wall tiles, to obtain a mirror finish. And the edges of large pieces, especially glazed and porcelain tiles, may be rectified to correct the variations in size of factory pieces, to the point of making them almost inappreciable, with a margin of error well below that stipulated by the norms.

FIXING

Wall and paving tiles are a finished product from an industrial standpoint, but from a functional or practical point of view, they are only a finished product once they are fixed on the wall, façade or floor. For this reason, the method of fixing is of great importance in the quality of the tiling. The laying of tiles on the floor is usually referred to as paving.

To obtain a quality covering, the support surface must meet the required conditions of stability, strength, flatness, evenness and cleanness. To this end, some preparatory treatment is necessary. On choosing the system of fixing and the fixing material the following factors should be taken into account: the target structure — walls, façades or floors — the type and size of ceramic tile and the support surface. Fixing generally involves the use of bonding materials that ensure the ceramic tiles stick to the surface. The decisive factor on choosing a bonding material is the adherence or bonding strength of the piece and the support surface.

The current tendency is to use the thin-bed process rather than the thick-set process with cement mortar and sand. The former employs materials suitable for all types of ceramic tile and support surfaces. The thin-bed process involves the use of cement-based adhesives or mortar glues, adhesive pastes and resin-based chemical adhesives. The choice depends on the type of ceramic tile (roughness of the underside and porosity). The adhesion of the bonding material may be physical, based on the penetration of the adhesive into the pores of the tile and the support surface, which creates a union. Cement adhesives work predominantly in this way and, consequently, they are suitable for fixing wall tiles, but not recommended for ceramic tiles with low or very low water absorption.

Chemical adhesion is produced by the formation of chemical bonds when the adhesive comes into contact with the tile and the support surface. It is typical of polymeric resin-based adhesives and is suitable for fixing very low porosity porcelain tiles. As well as the characteristics of the tile, it is necessary to take into account the nature of the supporting surface (brick or ceramic block; nogging or concrete subfloor; plaster finish or thin-coat plaster; ceramic covering or pre-existent terrazzo; timber; etc.). The manufacturers of bonding agents provide useful guidelines for choosing the right adhesive for each case, and on how to use them correctly: whether to apply adhesive to just the tile or to both the tile and the support surface. Once paving or tiling is finished, the joints between the pieces should be grouted using a cement paste or prefabricated mortar grouts.

There are other methods of fixing which are not meant to replace adhesives, but rather present new solutions for specific spaces or purposes. Thus, there is a mixed fixing method which involves the use of mortar glues together with a system of mechanical ties — bolts or nails which are driven into the supporting surface. This is used for cladding façades and roofs, such as on A. Isozaki's Palau Sant Jordi, in Barcelona, Spain.

Dry fixing consists of attaching the pieces to a steel framework fixed to the supporting surface. This is used to construct ventilated façades, whose features are the supporting surface, a layer of sound and thermal insulation, the metal substructure, the air space and the ceramic tiles. The roof of the Centenal Hall, in Nara, Japan, also by A. Isozaki, was clad using this technique, and also the façade of Caruso St. John's Art Gallery in Walsall, UK. More recently a system of dry fixing for floors has been developed; the ceramic tiles are supplied with a ribbed plastic backing which leaves a space on the underside for ventilation and drainage. This space may be also be used for electrical wiring, telephone installations and so on. Flanges on the edges of the plastic backing provide stability and allow the tiles to be removed to access the space underneath or replace damaged tiles.

WALL AND PAVING TILES AND THE ENVIRONMENT

Inevitably this production has an impact on the environment and there is a growing awareness of the need to reduce this impact to limits compatible with sustainable development.

    The Spanish ceramic tile industry devotes more and more attention to improving its environmental policies, during the whole manufacturing process from start to finish. To this end, it has taken measures that contribute to the protection and conservation of the environment by reducing the consumption of natural resources and cutting down on the discharge of waste products into the atmosphere, water and soil. The number of firms with ISO 14001 or EMAS certificates is growing, and a Spanish firm was the first to receive the EU Ecolabel.

    Amongst the measures taken for this purpose, the generalisation since 1990 of the single firing production process should be mentioned, using natural gas as fuel, the cleanest source of thermal energy currently available. In addition, by applying strict energy-efficient measures, the consumption of natural gas is reduced and the level of emissions of waste gases (in particular CO_2) per square metre or per ton of the product is the lowest attainable using current technology. To help reduce global emissions and increase energy efficiency, the process of cogeneration of heat and electricity has been applied in the production phases where it is technically viable: the industry itself supplies half of its own electricity demand and recycles waste gases produced during production to generate it.

    Another important advance is the reuse or recycling of waste products, which has reached an average of over 80% of the total residues. In so doing, not only is the amount of waste destined to end up at waste disposal plants reduced, but also this saves a million tonnes of raw material per year, especially water and clay. The average consumption of water per square metre of the product is one third of the maximum amount recommended by the European standards for the industry.

    The ceramic tile industry is included in the provisions of Directive 96/61/CE, drawn up by the Commission, which covers the integrated prevention and control of pollution. Consequently, firms are legally obliged to apply an integrated environmental policy, which fixes the maximum limits for emissions, based on the use of the best available technology. This policy is periodically reviewed to incorporate the latest technological advances that will facilitate the further reduction of atmospheric, water and soil emissions.

8 Water recycling unit in ceramic tile plant, Spain

8

MANUEL GONZÁLEZ is Consultant for ASCER (Spanish Ceramic Tile Manufacturers' Association) and Spokesman for the AENOR, CEN and ISO Technical Advisory Committees for the Standardisation of Ceramic Tiles.

Apartments Building
Ljubljana, Eslovenia

This is a two-floor apartment block with fifteen separate flats, common entrance lobby, interior winter garden and exterior summer atrium. The surrounding garden isolates the building from other neighbouring free-standing single-apartment buildings. A short driveway from the road by the river leads to an entrance platform, which in turn leads to the front door of the block. The condominium is situated on the edge of the city centre. It is about 15 minutes walk along the river bank to the main square in the city centre.

The condominium is a group of fifteen apartments. Its basic volume is anarchic, partitioned and non-monolithic, a design which provides optimal illumination of all apartments and the connection of interior spaces with the exterior by means of large green terraces, self-contained balconies and winter gardens. The fragmentation of the basic volume follows the irregular rhythm of the volumes of the balconies. The balconies extend far out from the building over the surrounding garden. This fragmentation reaches its peak in the pixelated appearance of the façades, created by facing them with multi-coloured ceramic tiles, and the pre-dimensioned black metal frames, which link large windows and balconies of orange wood.

Two- and three-dimensional partitioning of the basic volume creates a wealth of micro environments and the condominium constantly changes its appearance depending on where it is viewed from. Owing to the size of the development and the surrounding buildings, the condominium cannot be seen as a complete unit. We can only catch glimpses between the neighbouring buildings, of which there are in fact quite a number. The result is to awaken the onlooker's interest, make him or her wonder what goes on in that bright yellow and black tile building with the big windows. Who lives there and in what conditions? Is that multi-apartment building a design for a new lifestyle? Is it very different from anywhere else in Ljubljana? What makes it a comfortable place to live in?

The apartments have an extensive open floor plan. They create a feeling of belonging and identification with "my house, my garden and my apartment". In the wintertime I sit with my neighbours on the benches in the winter garden, and in the summer I meet them in the atrium in front of the winter garden.

The entrance façade and the glass front door control access to the platform. It is a true oasis in the heart of the Trnovo suburbs. It is a place to relax and to enjoy. It needs a view from the top floor to put the condominium into perspective within the wider context of the city: a view of Ljubljana Castle, the River Ljubljanica, skyscrapers, the Ljubljana moor and the Krim hilltop in the distance.

Pixelation of the façade

The final appearance of the façade of the Condominium Trnovski Pristan was achieved through a process of pixelation: the aim was to achieve something which would seem unreal at first glance. We shifted the perception of the size of the building in the eyes of the observer (that is why the building initially seems strange) and, at the same time, we tried to establish a completely new constructive relationship between the building and its immediate surroundings.

The ample black frames of the large window openings interconnect, thus creating what looks like a structural framework for the building. They seem to fragment the volume of the building as if they were load-bearing structures supporting parts of it, which of course is not the case. Around this conspicuous structure of window frames, we used a light facing of ceramic tiles. Their pixelated aspect blurs the meeting points between the dark outlines of the windows and the bright, light ceramic facing itself.

By day, when the sunlight reflected in the windows makes the glass surfaces of this heavy-looking structure look even darker, the pixelating effect of the black ceramic tiles blurs the edges, blending them into the lighter ceramic facing. The effect is enhanced when the building is viewed from afar.

The brighter pixelation of the rest of the ceramic tiles, yellow in their majority, combines with the "natural pixelation" of the willow leaves and other greenery along the quay. Thus, the so-called "Salamander House" adapts to and generates a new context in its surroundings.

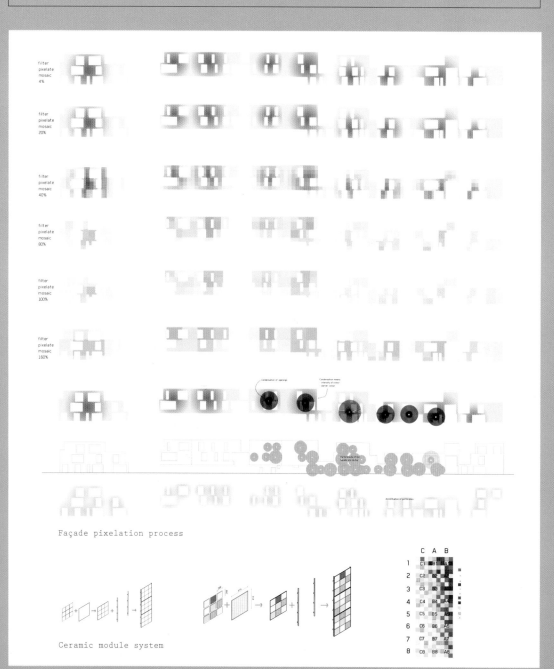

Façade pixelation process

Ceramic module system

Ground floor

0 1 2   5

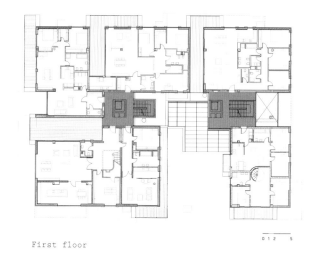

First floor

0 1 2   5

Second floor

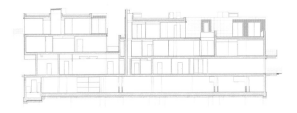

Long section

Cross section

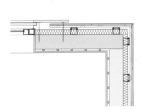

Façade horizontal
section detail

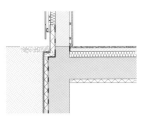

Façade vertical
section detail

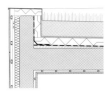

Roof section detail

ARCHITECTS: Sadar Vuga Arhitekti LOCATION: Trnovski
Pristan 22, Ljubljana, Slovenia DESIGN: 2002 CONSTRUCTION:
2004 DESIGN TEAM: Jurij Sadar and Boštjan Vuga with
Tina Hocevar, Miha Pešec, Tadej Žaucer, Mojca Kocbek
CLIENT: Begrad d.d., Novo Mesto CONTRACTOR: Begrad d.d.,
Novo Mesto STRUCTURAL ENGINEER: ELEA ELECTRICAL ENGINEER:
TE Biro MECANICAL ENGINEER: TE Biro LANDSCAPE DESIGN: SVA
+ Andrej Strgar u.d.i.ka TRAFFIC - SITE ENGINEER: Gašper
Blejec u.d.i.g. PHOTOGRAPHER: Ramon Prat

TILE: tiles 20 x 20 cm on an aluminium compound plate
61,6 x 61,6 x 1 cm, assembled as a ventilated façade

New Art Gallery and Public Square
Walsall, England

The Walsall Art Gallery has an in-situ concrete structure whose walls form the primary structure and define the main interior spaces of the building. The whole of the exterior of the shell is clad.

Onto the body of the tower is hung the outer layer of the rain screen, a more coarsely textured cloak of terracotta tiles whose scale reduces towards the top of the building. The tiles have a similar vertical proportion and the vertical joints shift in order to accommodate the internally determined window positions. The lapped bottom edge of the tiles and the corners of the building expose the 30 mm thickness of the extruded terracotta units. The 600 mm depth of the external wall is breached by windows formed with a welded stainless steel cage. The exterior of the cage is clad in mill finished stainless steel and flush structural glazing. The window cladding reinforces the impression of the stainless steel as an underlayer running beneath the building's ceramic overcloak.

The New Art Gallery is the home of the Garman Ryan Collection. The focus of the building is both its artistic programme and its wider cultural and educational role. The new building contains a suite of galleries for temporary exhibitions and events, in addition to the galleries for the permanent collection, extensive education facilities, conference room, bookshop and restaurant.

The Gallery is part of the regeneration of the east end of the town centre, around the canal arm and basin, previously used as an industrial wharf.

The new building is arranged as a tower at the head of the canal, giving it an appropriate prominence within the town. The tower form of the gallery makes possible a series of relatively small floors close to each other, with each having its own character and function. Some floors are grand, with high ceilings and an exposed roof structure and some are intimate, with lower ceilings and wall linings of timber and plaster. The diversity of facilities is reflected in an unusually wide range of atmospheres for a public building, evoking the pleasurable generosity of a big house.

The works of the Garman Ryan Collection are small scale, figurative and intimate, and the idea of the spatial organisation of the Gallery began with their accommodation within domestically scaled rooms. The rooms contain the themes of the permanent collection, and are gathered around a central hall on the first and second floors. All the spaces have windows, allowing visitors to look out over the town from the intimate environment of the gallery spaces: exhibition spaces, meeting rooms, spaces to relax and to work.

The façades of the tower are clad in pale terracotta **tiles** with a subtle natural colour variation. While the use of a clay cladding relates to the hard brick and terracotta common to all industrial and public buildings in the Midlands region, the surface of the building is fragile and thin, wrapping and disguising the complexity of the interior like the feathers of a bird. The dispersed pattern of flush windows and individual overlapping tiles is intended to give the building a surface of fine decoration such as is found in the lasting architecture of Victorian civic building.

The design of the public spaces around the gallery and canal was led by the artists Richard Wentworth and Catherine Yass. The public square is an inside-out square wrapping around the tower, whose bold pattern is seen from the windows above and whose stripes measure the distance to the horizon along the canal arm.

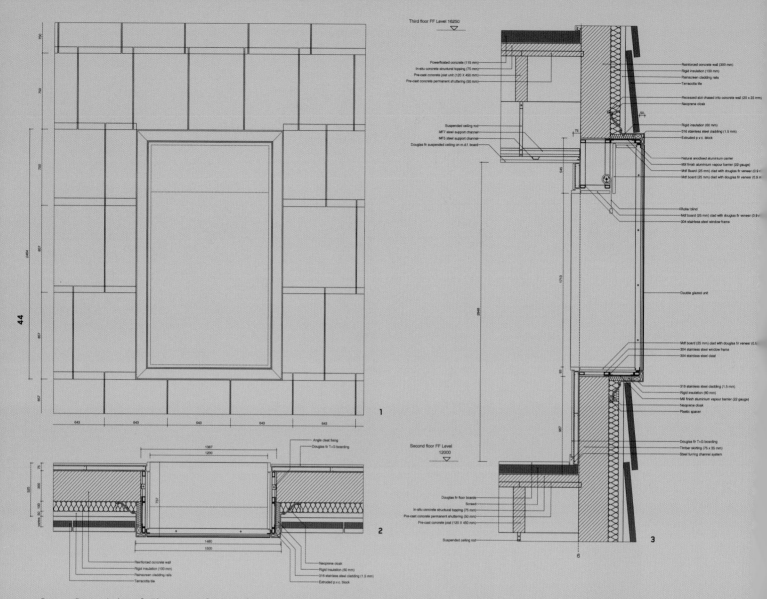

Third floor FF Level 16250

Powerfloated concrete (115 mm)
In-situ concrete structural topping (75 mm)
Pre-cast concrete joist unit (120 X 450 mm)
Pre-cast concrete permanent shuttering (50 mm)

Suspended ceiling rod
MF7 steel support channel
MF5 steel support channel
Douglas fir suspended ceiling on m.d.f. board

Reinforced concrete wall (300 mm)
Rigid insulation (100 mm)
Rainscreen cladding rails
Terracotta tile
Recessed slot chased into concrete wall (20 x 25 mm)
Neoprene cloak
Rigid insulation (60 mm)
316 stainless steel cladding (1.5 mm)
Extruded p.v.c. block
Natural anodised aluminium barrier
Mill finish aluminium vapour barrier (22 gauge)
Mdf Board (25 mm) clad with douglas fir veneer (0.9 r
Mdf board (25 mm) clad with douglas fir veneer (0.9 m
Roller blind
Mdf board (25 mm) clad with douglas fir veneer (0.9 r
304 stainless steel window frame
Double glazed unit
Mdf board (25 mm) clad with douglas fir veneer (0.5
304 stainless steel window frame
304 stainless steel cleat
316 stainless steel cladding (1.5 mm)
Rigid insulation (60 mm)
Mill finish aluminium vapour barrier (22 gauge)
Neoprene cloak
Plastic spacer
Douglas fir T+G boarding
Timber skirting (75 x 35 mm)
Steel furring channel system

Second floor FF Level 12000

Douglas fir floor boards
Screed
In-situ concrete structural topping (75 mm)
Pre-cast concrete permanent shuttering (50 mm)
Pre-cast concrete joist (120 X 450 mm)
Suspended ceiling rod

Angle cleat fixing
Douglas fir T+G boarding

Reinforced concrete wall
Rigid insulation (100 mm)
Rainscreen cladding rails
Terracotta tile
Neoprene cloak
Rigid insulation (60 mm)
316 stainless steel cladding (1.5 mm)
Extruded p.v.c. block

Garman Ryan window: **1** Elevation, **2** Plan, **3** Section

Second floor

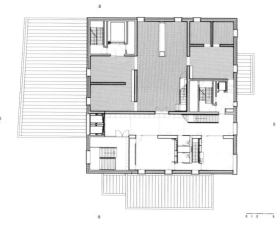

First floor

Mezzanine floor

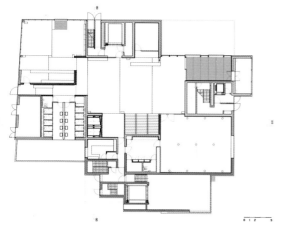

Ground floor

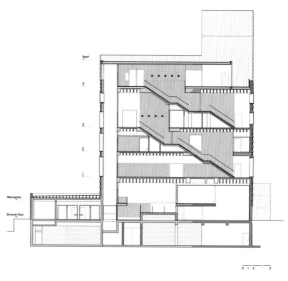

Section CC

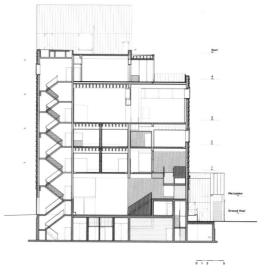

Section DD

ARCHITECTS: Caruso St John Architects
LOCATION: The New Art Gallery Walsall, Gallery Square, WS2 8LG Walsall, England **DESIGN:** 1995 (competition)
CONSTRUCTION: 2000 **DESIGN TEAM:** Adam Caruso and Peter St John with Martin Bradley, Laurie Hallows, Alun Jones, Andrés Martinez, Silvia Ullmayer
CLIENT: Walsall Metropolitan Borough Council **PROJECT DIRECTOR:** Peter Jenkinson, Creative Partnerships
MAIN CONTRACTOR: Sir Robert McAlpine Ltd **QUANTITY SURVEYOR:** Hanscomb **STRUCTURAL ENGINEER:** Ove Arup and Partners **SERVICES ENGINEER:** Ove Arup and Partners
FAÇADE CONSULTANT: Arup Façade Engineering **ACOUSTIC CONSULTANT:** Arup Acoustics **PLANNING SUPERVISOR:** Ove Arup and Partners **ACCESS:** David Bonnett Architects
LANDSCAPE ARCHITECT: Lynn Kinnear **GRAPHIC DESIGN:** Michael Nash and Jane **ARTISTS:** Richard Wentworth, Catherine Yass **PHOTOGRAPHERS:** Hélène Binet, Gary Kirkham (façade in contruction)

TILE: these terracotta tiles were made specially for the project
DIMENSIONS: the size of the tiles ranges from 60 x 100 cm to about 40 x 60 cm, decreasing in size as they go up the building.

Museum of Tiles Manolo Safont
Onda, Spain

Anyone who knows Onda will understand why a huge open portal has been designed to create a museum. In addition, anyone who knows the site itself will understand the reason for the dimensions of this portal, its alignment, and why it is accessible from both sides.

And visitors may well be surprised to find that, on reaching the threshold, a wall in diagonal guides them from one jamb to the other without ever abandoning the confines of the portal.

On the entrance floor, within the boundaries described above, visitors will find an information point before entering the area of Temporary Exhibitions, situated exceptionally inside the portal and laid out as an introduction to the area of Permanent Exhibitions. On the way back, on leaving, they will find a projection hall. Beyond that, back in the lobby, they will reemerge by some small shops and the washrooms.

A wide accessible ramp ascends from the lobby to the upper floor where the bar and restaurant located under the lintel of the portal afford privileged views of the local castle and the sea in the distance. The conference hall is also situated on this floor.

The ground floor also provides access to the lower floors. Administration, the research area, the board room, the area reserved for friends of the museum, and the teaching facilities are situated on the first lower floor.

The auxiliary staff room, the curators' offices, the restoration area and the entrance to storerooms, workshops and the mechanical equipment room are located on the next floor down.

The storerooms are reached by a ramp, suitable for parking, situated at the rear. A street that descends perpendicularly to this ramp provides access. There is also an exit out of the precinct on the lowest part of the site.

Ceramic materials have been used to clad the interior and the exterior of the Museum.

The large area of the entrance floor was paved with 33 x 33 cm stoneware with a rustic finish. For the lower ground floor, 45 x 45 cm stoneware was used. The bathrooms are decorated with 15 x 15 cm white and blue glazed wall tiles.

A combination of distinct textures and colours was used for the exterior finish. The design consists of ventilated façades clad with two types of porcelain stoneware. The lower half is clad with 60 x 120 cm tiles with a rough finish. For the upper half 60 x 120 cm tiles with a polished finished have been used. Other exteriors, such as various perimeter walls, are clad with the same tile, but in a smaller 30 x 60 cm format and laid with staggered joints.

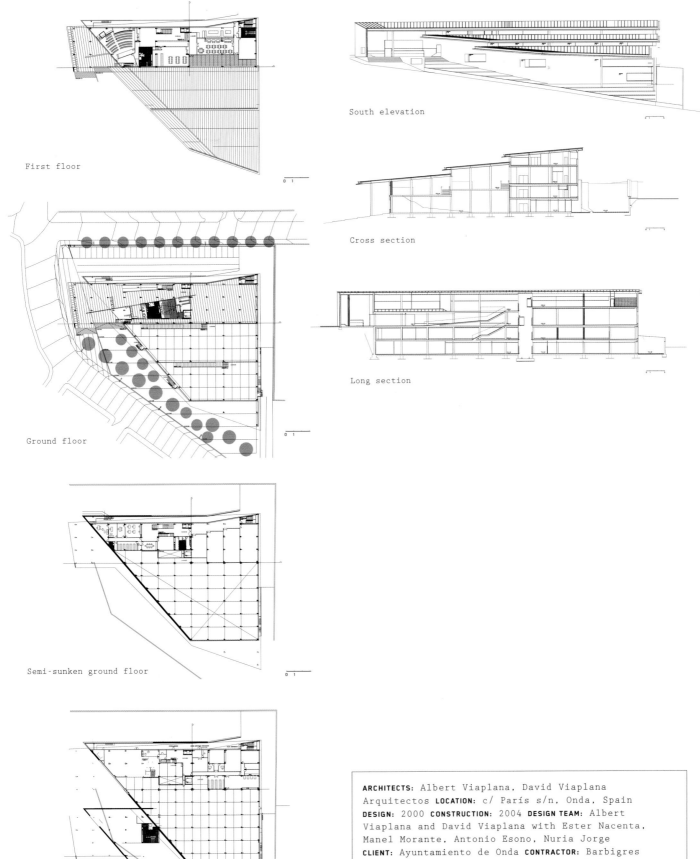

First floor

Ground floor

Semi-sunken ground floor

Basement

South elevation

Cross section

Long section

ARCHITECTS: Albert Viaplana, David Viaplana Arquitectos **LOCATION:** c/ París s/n, Onda, Spain **DESIGN:** 2000 **CONSTRUCTION:** 2004 **DESIGN TEAM:** Albert Viaplana and David Viaplana with Ester Nacenta, Manel Morante, Antonio Esono, Nuria Jorge **CLIENT:** Ayuntamiento de Onda **CONTRACTOR:** Barbigres Mediterraneo S.A. **STRUCTURAL ENGINEERING:** Luis Moya **SERVICES ENGINEER:** GCA ingenieros

TILE: porcelain tile for the façade and glazed stoneware tiles in various formats for the interior

House 4C
Barcelona, Spain

A pair of houses in a garden, dating from the first third of the last century, had to be converted into a modern urban living-unit. It was decided to keep the original perimeter wall at the back of the smallish plot because this allowed the conservation of the old raised garden in the sunshine at the front, which overlooks the drive and affords fine views of Barcelona. There was a garage through a basement at street level, which provided access to the ground floor and the garden.

The project, rather than recurring to sophisticated solutions, makes sensible use of technology. It does not include, from this standpoint, any special technical details except those dealing with practical difficulties in its execution and the proposal for the restoration of the main façades. These consisted of a single sheet of common brick rendered with lime plaster and plastered on the interior. Once the new window arrangements were completed, a ventilated façade was designed which covers the old exterior and accommodates the necessary layer of insulation, both giving the façade a new look and updating it with the latest technology.

To this end we designed a stoneware tile fixed by stainless steel ties to the existing brick. The ties are concealed because they support the piece by means of bolts which are lodged laterally inside the piece.

These ties were fixed directly to the wall, or to vertical battens when it was necessary to leave a free space within the wall to accommodate the sliding sashes of certain French windows.

The jambs, sills and lintels of the windows were resolved by a frame of 6 mm thick galvanised plate.

The tile itself meets the specifications for the design of façades. The piece is stoneware fired at 1,200°C with an intermediate chamber. It is just 4 cm thick. This material was chosen for its extremely high quality, texture and visual impact, and also because its inevitable tendency to warp distinguishes it from the cold perfection of similar claddings. The design is based on a precise organisation of volumes, which are enriched by the above-mentioned irregularity.

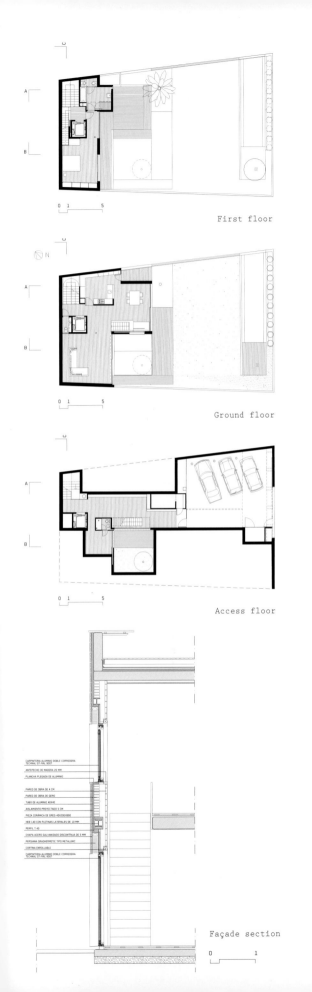

First floor

Ground floor

Access floor

Façade section

CARPINTERIA ALUMINIO DOBLE CORREDERA
TECHNAL STI RAL 9007

ANTEPECHO DE MADERA 20 MM

PLANCHA PLEGADA DE ALUMINIO

PARED DE OBRA DE X CM

PARED DE OBRA DE GERO

TUBO DE ALUMINIO 40X40

AISLAMIENTO PROYECTADO 5 CM

PIEZA CERÁMICA DE GRES 40X200X890

HEB 140 CON PLETINAS LATERALES DE 10 MM

PERFIL T 40

CHAPA ACERO GALVANIZADO DISCONTINUA DE 5 MM

PERSIANA GRADHERMETIC TIPO METALUNIC

CORTINA ENROLLABLE

CARPINTERIA ALUMINIO DOBLE CORREDERA
TECHNAL STI RAL 9007

0   1

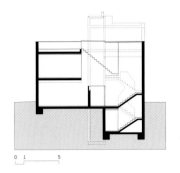

Section C

0 1   5

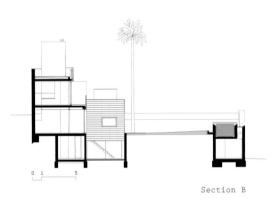

Section B

0 1   5

Section A

0 1   5

ARCHITECTS: Jaume Bach arquitectes **LOCATION:** c/ Quatre
Camins 5-7, Barcelona, Spain **DESIGN:** 1996 **CONSTRUCTION:**
2003 **DESIGN TEAM:** Jaume Bach with Eugeni Bach,
Anna Bach, Núria Bartomeu, Joan Pallàs **TECHNICAL
ARCHITECT:** Joan Surís, Francesc Xairó **CLIENT:** private
CONTRACTOR: COMSA **STRUCTURAL ENGINEER:** Robert Brufau i
Associats **PHOTOGRAPHER:** Lluís Casals

TILE: stoneware cladding for ventilated façades
DIMENSIONS: 90 x 20 x 4 cm

Award-winner in the 2nd Edition of Tile of Spain
Awards of Architecture and Interior Design (2003-2004)

New Headquarters of the Royal Nautical Club
Tarragona, Spain

The whole development consists of a new spatial arrangement of platforms in the area of the yachting marina, and its integration may be viewed as a change in the layout of the port.

This new layout consists of an elevated platform which is the focus of the club's main social activities, and it is ideally placed to afford dominant views of the yachting marina itself, the port entrance, the future beach to the west, and the horizon.

Part of this platform, situated on a level with the top of the western breakwater, is within the interior of the main building while the remainder consists of an exterior terrace and solarium surrounding the swimming pools, plus the main balcony which overlooks the port.

The situation and alignment of the building meets the dual need to segregate a space within the yachting marina for the use of the Nautical Club and to take maximum advantage of the fact that, on the upper level, it faces towards both the yachting marina and the western beach.

The roof of the main building is not included in these considerations, but its simple solid volume is precisely what gives this building its emblemtic character. This roof overhangs one side of the building to generate a large doorway facing the principal pedestrian walkway in the port. It serves as the main access to the Club and the western beach.

The offices (Port Authority and club administration), changing rooms, archives and machine rooms are located in the basement of the buildings, and also an extra space reserved for future activities.

The whole development is divided into two clearly differentiated units: on the one hand the main building and, on the other, the swimming pool complex.

The main building is designed on two levels. The administrative centre, subdivided into two sections, the Port Authority and the club offices, is located on the ground floor. The upper floor accommodates the more representative activities of the institution and is linked directly to the swimming pool building by the bar terrace. The swimming pool complex is a unit basically providing sports facilities and services for the main building.

The construction of an indoor "fronton" court is also planned, in juxtaposition with the eastern breakwater. This will help to block out indiscreet views of the swimming pool and thus give the complex a greater degree of privacy and seclusion.

Why stoneware? The roof of the Nautical Club of Tarragona is notable for its lightness and denotes the "piano nobile" of the building, the most emblematic part of the institution.

At variance with the tectonic solemnity of the materials used on the ground floor, the roof was designed to show its affinity with nautical architecture, not so much as regards the materials actually used, but rather as conveyed by the intrinsic qualities of this type of construction: the predominance of white, the sheen of the covering, the stainless materials — features that remind one of glazed ceramics.

All our requisites were met by gloss white stoneware, and the large dimensions of the tiles suited the large scale of the roof.

Its use on the three façades of the portico ensures a diaphanous effect when viewed from higher up.

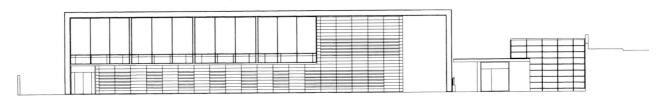

Long section

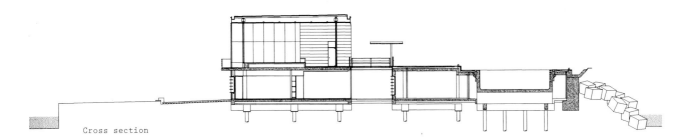

Cross section

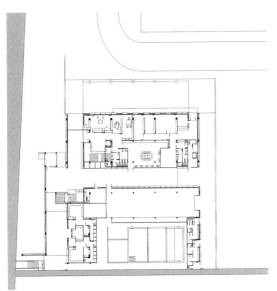

First floor

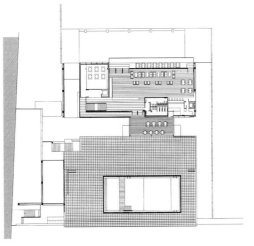

Ground floor

ARCHITECTS: Baena Casamor Quera Arquitectes **LOCATION:** Moll de Costa, Port s/n, Tarragona, Spain **DESIGN:** 1995 (competition) **CONSTRUCTION:** 1997 **DESIGN TEAM:** David Baena, Carles Casamor and José Maria Quera with Cruz Lacoma **CONSTRUCTION SURVEYORS:** Joan Anton Díaz, Manuel Díaz **CLIENT:** Reial Club Nàutic de Tarragona **CONTRACTOR:** Dragados **STRUCTURAL ENGINEER:** Manuel Arguijo **SERVICES ENGINEERS:** Miquel Portell **PHOTOGRAPHER:** Jordi Bernadó

TILE: glazed stoneware tiles
DIMENSIONS: 60 x 90 cm

Ventilated ceramic tile façades: advantages and anchoring systems

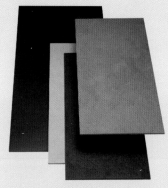

A

B

A and B Porcelain stoneware tiles

The use of ceramic tiles in architecture has been a common practice for a long time. Without going back very far in time we can recall the splendid use that the masters of Modernism made of it. However, from the end of WWII the situation changed radically.

There were, in our judgment, two main causes for the decline in the use of ceramic tiles in architecture. The first was the industrialization of construction processes, which meant a less demand for artisanal work and thus a decline in the number of adequately trained craftsmen. This led to a widespread problem of faulty fitting of tiles. The second cause was the emergence of the International Style, which banished tiles to the interiors of buildings. Subsequent attempts to use tiles as an outer skin had, in many cases, disappointing results, among other reasons because improvements in the quality of ceramic tiles also entailed a significant decrease in their porosity, which meant a loss in the adherence of traditional cement mortars, and thus shedding tiles.

Fortunately, the situation has changed for the better and today we have wholly reliable fitting systems, enabling us to predict a brilliant future for ceramic tiles in architecture.

We can classify these fitting systems in three clearly differentiated groups:

* Direct adherence
* Mechanical anchoring systems
* Mixed anchoring systems

The direct adherence fitting systems use cement-based adhesives with a high proportion of mixed bonding agents. As opposed to the traditional cement-and-sand mortars, the adherence of which is fundamentally mechanical, this type of adhesive guarantees a high level of chemical adherence with low-porosity tiles such as porcelain stoneware. The recommended fitting technique is with a thin layer of double-spread gluing. These adhesives provide excellent adherence and, if applied correctly, ensure perfect fitting.

On the other hand, mechanical anchoring systems use more or less complex mechanisms to fix ceramic pieces to surfaces. Below we analyze in greater detail the different types of anchoring systems available on the market and their suitability for ventilated façades.

Finally, the mixed systems combine the previous two, and are always used with ceramic pieces larger than 40 x 60 cm or weighing more than 40 Kg/m^2. The mechanical anchoring systems are usually clamps screwed into the spaces between pieces that have been previously fitted with adhesives.

ADVANTAGES OF VENTILATED FAÇADES

This type of façade incorporates an air gap to provide ventilation, which in turn offers significant energy savings. The basic scheme of a façade of this type (**1**), with its standard parts, includes (1: bearing wall, 2: insulation, 3: substructure and 4: tiling), although depending on the type of system it may include other components. Below we analyse some of the advantages of these façades.

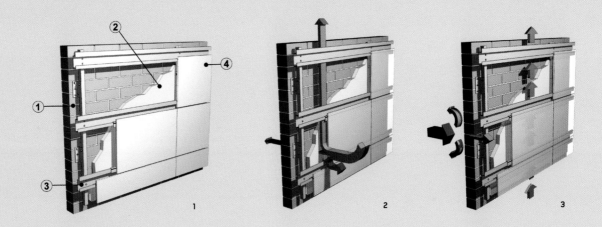

Thermal insulation The first obstacle to heat penetrating from the outside is the outer skin, part of which it reflects away from the building. The remaining heat heats the air in the gap, causing a fall in density, and the air rises due to the chimney effect. Behind this ventilated air gap, the heat encounters a third barrier in the form of the insulation covering the enclosing wall. The effectiveness of this series of layers is such that only a small part of the heat received by the outer skin reaches the interior of the building (**2**).
The façade works in reverse in winter. The higher temperature is inside the building and the barriers that it encounters as it tries to escape are the wall and the insulation. The rising air inside the air gap carries away moisture, helping to keep the insulation dry and improving its performance (**3**).

Elimination of condensation With any façade the difference in air temperature between the two sides of the enclosure produces a heat flow from the warmer side (normally interior) to the cooler side (normally exterior). And we also know that atmospheric air contains a certain amount of moisture that condenses at dew point. Thus, under humid conditions, it is advisable to avoid having any points of the enclosure where the temperature is below the dew point. On the ventilated façades these conditions are met naturally, as we have seen previously. On one hand, the temperature difference between the outer face of the insulation and the inner face of the enclosure is less than with non-ventilated façades, while the rising air removes excess moisture from the insulation (**4**).

Elimination of Thermal Bridges Continuous insulation on the wall is an effective measure against thermal bridges that form on the edges of slabs and perimeter columns (**5**).

Water Protection The air gap creates a separation between the outer skin of the ventilated façade and the outer face of the insulation, which protects it from water. The flow of water can affect the outer surface of the insulation (**6**).

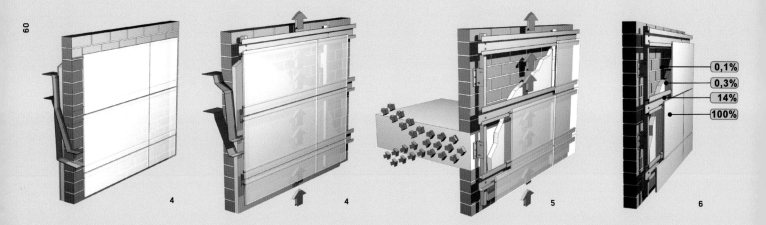

Advantages of porcelain stoneware on ventilated façades Although the suitability of ceramic tiles for covering exterior surfaces is evidenced in a long architectural tradition, its performance compared with other materials commonly used on façades needed to be tested scientifically. Thus, the company TAU Cerámica commissioned an independent laboratory to do a study comparing the performance of porcelain stoneware and traditional materials. The following table contains a summary of the results of the study.

The columns show the score for each material in the tests in the rows (the higher the score the better the performance). The marbles are White Macael and Red Alicante; the limestones Crema Marfil and Black Marquina; the granites White Crystal and Pink Porriño. The timber is timber veneer over laminated plastic. The last three columns correspond to laminated plastic, lacquered aluminium polyethylene core composite and concrete shield, all for exterior uses.

The rows show the tests to which the materials were submitted, along with the standardized procedures followed in each test. In the case of moisture expansion the samples were submerged in water for seven days at ambient temperature. The stain-resistance test had to be defined since there was no standardized procedure to apply. Two staining agents were chosen: the first by impregnation (rhodamine solution 0.1 g/L) and

		Materials								
		Porcelain		Marble	Limestone	Granite	Timber	Plastic	Lacquered Aluminium	Concrete
		Natural	Polished							
Dimensional characteristics	UNE-EN ISO 10545-2	HIGH	HIGH	HIGH	HIGH	HIGH	HIGH	HIGH	MEDIUM	MEDIUM
Bending resistance	UNE-EN ISO 10545-4	HIGH	HIGH	HIGH	HIGH	HIGH	HIGH	HIGH	LOW	HIGH
Frost resistance	UNE-EN ISO 10545-12	HIGH	HIGH	HIGH	HIGH	HIGH	HIGH	HIGH	HIGH	LOW
Permeability	BS 4131	HIGH	HIGH	MEDIUM	MEDIUM	MEDIUM	MEDIUM	MEDIUM	HIGH	LOW
Mass/surface ratio		MEDIUM	MEDIUM	LOW	LOW	LOW	MEDIUM	MEDIUM	HIGH	LOW
Moisture expansion		HIGH	HIGH	HIGH	HIGH	LOW	LOW	LOW	MEDIUM	MEDIUM
Linear thermal expansion	UNE-EN ISO 10545-8	HIGH	HIGH	LOW	HIGH	HIGH	LOW	LOW	LOW	MEDIUM
Stain resistance		HIGH	HIGH	LOW	HIGH	LOW	HIGH	HIGH	MEDIUM	LOW
Salt spray corrosion	UNE 112017 ISO 9227	HIGH	HIGH	LOW	HIGH	HIGH	HIGH	HIGH	HIGH	LOW
Atmosphere SO2	UNE-EN ISO 6988	HIGH	HIGH	LOW	LOW	MEDIUM	MEDIUM	HIGH	HIGH	LOW
Solar ageing	UNE-EN ISO 11341 (M2, C-A)	HIGH	HIGH	LOW	LOW	MEDIUM	LOW	MEDIUM	MEDIUM	MEDIUM

source: TAU Cerámica

the second superficial action (black permanent marker). The cleaning products were commercial bleach (35gr CL2/L) for the impregnation and trichloroethylene (99%) for the superficial action. A mechanical cleaning device was used so that the pressure applied was equal in all cases and finally the Lab chromatic coordinates for before and after cleaning were compared.

The table shows that the porcelain stoneware tiles perform as well as or better than other materials commonly used on façades.

ANCHORING SYSTEMS ON VENTILATED CERAMIC TILE FAÇADES

Below we describe the most common types of anchoring systems for ceramic tiles on ventilated façades. The systems are classified according to whether they are visible or not. With the exception of the last (adjustable anchoring), all use a substructure. These systems are for dry pressed and extruded tiles, and they all require some sort of supplementary system to prevent lateral movement of the tiles. It should be noted that most of these systems are protected by patents or utility models. The following scheme shows the classification for the described systems.

C and D Hotels. Ventilated façades clad with ceramic tiles. Photos: Porcelanosa and Tau Cerámica

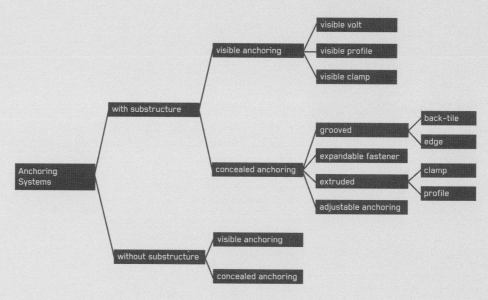

Visible bolt In this system, the tiles are fixed to the façade with four bolts, one at each corner. The bolts are screwed into flanges on the posts, with rubber strips to prevent tile vibration.

The system is adaptable to the dimensions of the tiles: horizontally, adjusting the spacing between posts according to the width of the tile, and vertically, drilling out the flanges according to the height (**7**).

Visible profile Thanks to the form of the extruded components of the post, the façade tiles are pinned lengthwise between the vertical flanges. Two rubber strips fitted between the flanges on the post, and in contact with the tile, impede vertical slippage of the tile and vibration caused by wind (**8**).

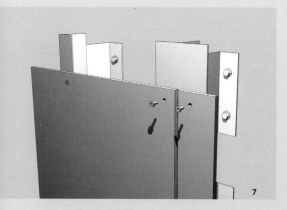
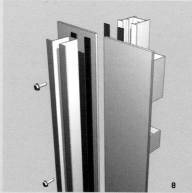

Visible clamp This system uses a clamp fitted at each point where four tiles meet, securing the two lower pieces while securing and bearing the two upper pieces.

With this system, it is advisable to apply a bead of monocomponent polyurethane putty during fitting to prevent tile vibration due to wind. This system is highly versatile in terms of the arrangement of the anchoring systems, according to the needs of the project, and can be used with tiles of different thicknesses (**9**).

An especially ingenious variation consists of a clamp that incorporates a tab to facilitate fitting and removal of tiles (**10**).

Grooved-back tile The anchoring consists of the incorporation of a special section of aluminium profile on the upper and lower part of the tile, in a groove running from top to bottom, with a maximum depth of 30% of the thickness on a 45º angle.

The tile is anchored by means of the aluminium profile at the top and bottom for equal transmission of loads on the aluminium substructure and to permit expansion. In manufacturing an elastic is fitted between the aluminium and tile to join them (**11**).

There are variations on this system with two grooves in the upper and two in lower part of the tile (**12**).

E Refurbished housing estate. Ventilated façade clad with ceramic tiles by Pamesa

F Ventilated façade clad with ceramic tiles by Roca

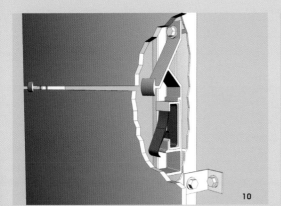

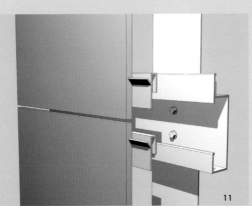

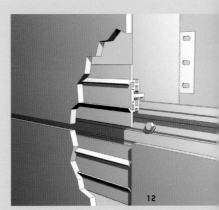

Another effective system uses four flexible steel clips inserted in the corners of the tile. The two elements are joined mechanically, with two V-shaped incisions at each corner of the back of tile, into which the clip is fitted. The clips fit into the horizontal profiles of the substructure, to provide stable anchorage for the tile on the façade (**13**).

Grooved edge The anchoring consists of clamps that fix the tile by upper and lower grooves to a substructure solely of vertical posts. The groove may run the entire length or only parts of the edge. One clamp holds two tiles, fitted into the upper groove of the lower tile and into the lower groove of the upper one (**14** and **15**).

Expandable fastener The respective fastening pieces (clamps, bearing profiles) are mounted at the fastening points of the tile (corners) with an integrated stainless steel bolt. The fastening pieces are

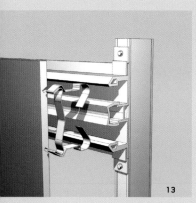
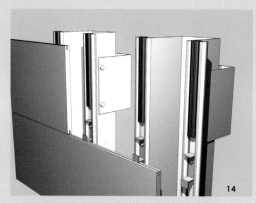
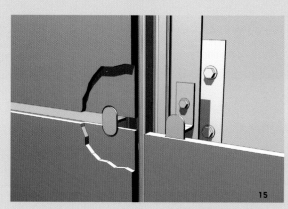

fixed with self-locking steel nut. A neoprene gasket is fitted between the fastening pieces and the base structure (**16**). A variation on this system uses overlapping tiles (**17**). This arrangement can be found in other systems such as visible clamp and bolt.

Anchoring systems for extruded pieces In this case we find two systems: In the first, the extruded tiles come with grooves at the top and bottom and are fixed with stainless steel claws riveted to the aluminium base structure. To control vibration due to wind load, a press-fitted "gasket profile" is used. The section of the pieces is such that they do not need any machining after manufacturing (**18**).

In the second case the tiles are fixed vertically at two points along the section, a few centimetres from the top and the bottom, with T-shaped aluminium profiles inserted in the grooves on the tiles. The profiles are fixed to an aluminium substructure of posts and cross-pieces, in turn bolted to the building (**19**).

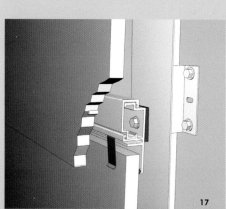
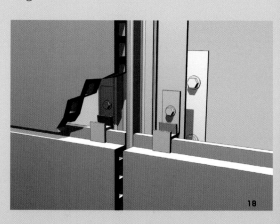

Visible anchoring without substructure The anchoring system is an intermediate element between the structure of the building and its façade, without the need for a substructure. The system is adjustable in three dimensions (axes x, y and z), without putting stress on the tiles, to achieve the correct position, alignment and flushness. Since the element is independent, it can be positioned on the façade freely, making the system adaptable to different sizes and the variations in the joints between tiles (**20**).

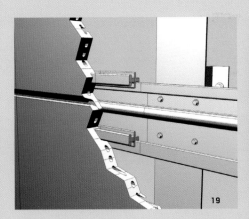 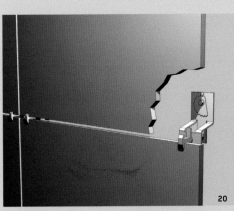 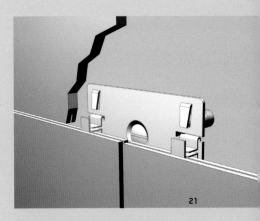

Concealed anchoring without substructure This system consists solely of an anchoring between the structure of the building and the tile enclosure. The anchoring, made of stainless steel, is designed to fix tiles of variable thickness vertically and horizontally. The fastener consists of a double piece that, on the one hand, anchors and levels the tile to the structure of the building and, on the other, from which hang the tiles by their two pre-grooved sides, which are also held by mobile tabs that press against the tile and the support to dampen vibration (**21**).

JAVIER MIRA PEIDRO is a technical architect (Polytechnic University of Valencia). He has been a member ALICER since its founding in April 1993. Currently he is the Association's vice director and directs its Architecture Department.
He is coordinator of nine ceramic tile R+D projects, related to design, architectural applications and innovative decorative processes.
He has published several articles in scientific or technical journals and the specialized press for the sector.
He has given numerous conferences at several congresses.
He has won four prizes for his projects from Spanish and international design competitions.

Fish Market
Port of Benicarló, Spain

This building has its origins in the public competition of preliminary projects for the construction of a fish market and the reorganisation of the surroundings of the port in Benicarló. The proposed solution was based on the concept of the Mediterranean market. Due to some confusion between the original idea and the actual project, which required a solution contrary to the original proposals, the project was stopped two months before the construction was completed.

Sited on the central quay and on the built-up limits of the town centre, the building is designed to make its mark as an infrastructure which agglutinates the sale and distribution of fish in the vicinity. The building is conceived on two scales, that of the structure itself and that of the users.

The shell (22.5 x 57.4 x 10.5 m) consists of a perimeter structure of porticos of regular size covered by prefabricated beams with a 20 m span, thus creating an uninterrupted roof visible from all parts of the site. Offices, stores, cold-storage rooms, lobbies and the auctioning tiers are laid out within this volume.

The façade, designed as an continuous envelop, is intended to provide adequate air-conditioning in the interior in the height of summer. It aims for an acceptable degree of comfort through the provision of shade and controlled of air circulation. This element was designed as an arrangement of two separate walls mounted on two peripheral rows of galvanised steel tubular columns, stretching from the base wall to the crown of the façade. The interior is divided into two parts; the lower area is glazed in to protect users from the wind and the upper area is enveloped by a thick mesh of plastified steel to prevent birds from entering. The outer shell consists of a lattice which affords protection against the sun. It is also intended to contain and delimit the general space and allows certain restricted views. The lattice is formed by sections of galvanised steel, anchored to the base wall which is clad with ceramic pieces. The openings of the building consist of a number of large, well-placed windows, framed by a casing of concrete and spanning the width of the façades.

It is the light reflected by the sea and the ceramics, and filtered by the latticework, which unexpectedly illuminates the interior walls and exposes areas veiled in shadow.

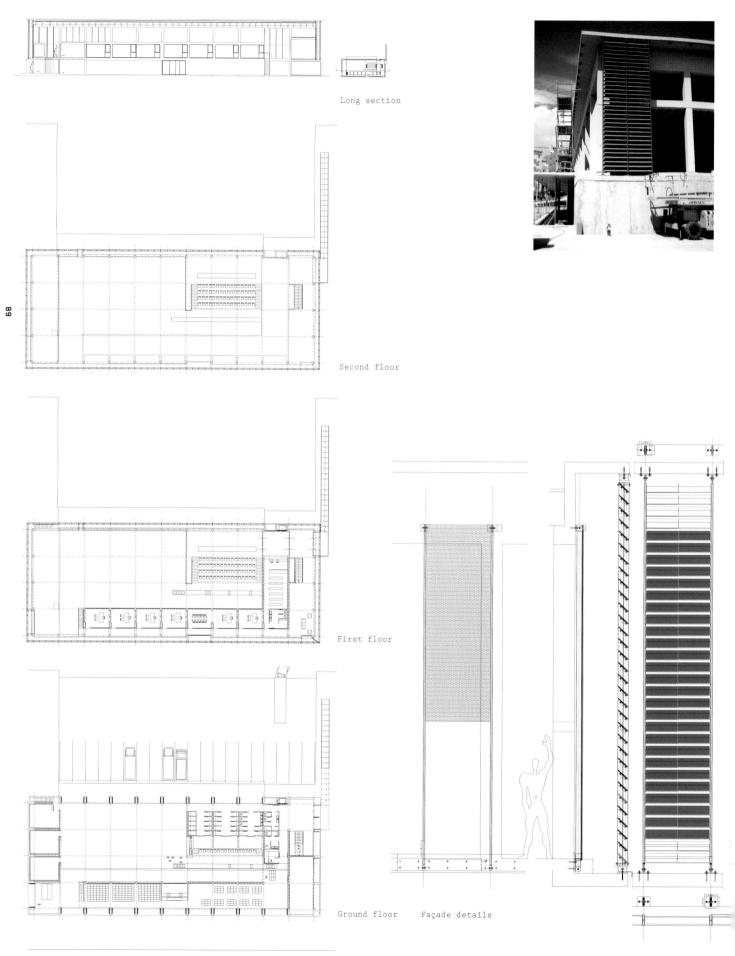

Long section

Second floor

First floor

Ground floor   Façade details

ARCHITECTS: Eduardo de Miguel and José María Urzelai
LOCATION: Puerto de Benicarló, Spain DESIGN: 1996
(competition) FIRST PROJECT: 1997 FINAL PROJECT: 2001
CONSTRUCTION: 2002-2004 CONSTRUCTION SURVEYOR: David
Navarro CLIENT: Consellería de Infraestructuras y
Transporte, Generalitat Valenciana STRUCTURAL ENGINEER:
Typsa CONTRACTOR: Cyes

TILE: extruded ceramic tile
DIMENSIONS: 59,2 x 27,2 x 1,5 cm

35 Living Units
Badalona, Spain

Badalona is a city with an important industrial tradition whose urban growth was the result of heavy immigration after the Spanish Civil War and the arrival of new industries.

The city's appearance is characterised by the array of ceramic party walls of varying height, designed in keeping with the techniques of their corresponding periods.

The project is adapted to the outlines of one of the old factories, one of the original buildings in the neighbourhood (1940) and still partly conserved as a tribute and a reminder of another epoch. The project maintains the original façade, in the manner of a "container". On the other hand, the building is now used for a very different purpose to the original margarine and chocolate factory: it has been converted into 35 living units.

Particular attention has been paid to the areas of transition between the city and the living units: scattered common areas such as walkways, halls, staircases, lifts, corridors, etc.

The façade was built using a dry covering in which materials manufactured for other purposes were recycled conceptually for a new use. In this case large-dimension ceramic lintels were transformed into 1,590 flowerpots/window boxes. The window box is the unit which, by force of repetition, generates the building's final form. In the traditional manner, garden plants have been placed in them (wild species which are self-regulating). This vegetation gives the interior a human scale which is "transmitted" to the city. At the same time, the building will function like a biotope and be gradually colonised by its new inhabitants.

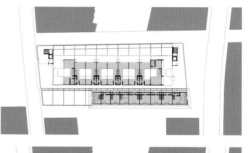

Second floor

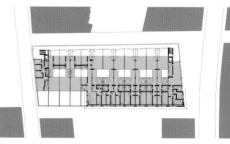

First floor

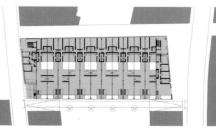

Ground floor

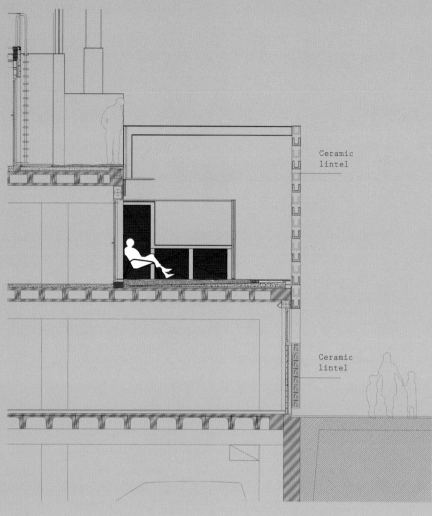

Ceramic
lintel

Ceramic
lintel

Section

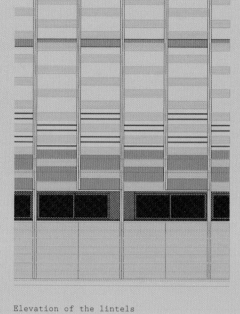

Elevation of the lintels

Plan of the lintels

Lintel details

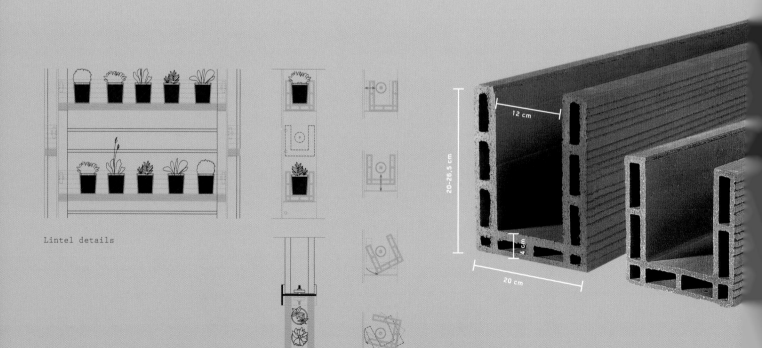

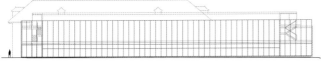

Elevations

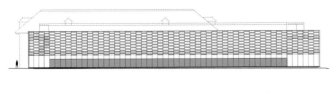

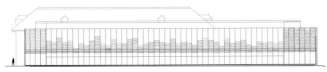

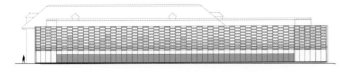

ARCHITECT: Toni Gironès LOCATION: c/ General Weyler 253, Badalona, Spain DESIGN: 2001-2002 CONSTRUCTION: 2003-2005 DESIGN TEAM: Toni Gironès with Roger Mayol, Sergio Perez, Ines Sobral, Jordi Portal CONSTRUCTION SURVEYOR: Angel Gil CLIENT: IFGSA CONTRACTOR: AEJ (concrete structure), Construcciones Juanes STRUCTURAL ENGINEER: BIS arquitectes AGRICULTURAL ENGINEER: Teresa Gal·lí Izard PHOTOGRAPHER: Toni Gironès

CERAMIC ELEMENT: lintels
DIMENSIONS: 20 x 20 x 110 cm

Refuge in the Hills
Ciudad Real, Spain

Just a few kilometres from Ciudad Real, on the north side of a low sierra which dominates the irrigated plain of the Vicario, the possibility came about to build a house; something small and unambitious for the weekends. Due to the low budget and the fact that the house was commissioned by sensitive trusting clients, it was projected as a sort of open refuge, serving as protection from the elements, but simultaneously allowing the occupants to perceive nature in all its splendour. The design throws all its creative tension into a simple, but intense relationship, house-water-tree, through the complete exposure of a sole space. The idea is to search for sensations allied to the natural environment, from within a warm shelter whose material austerity precludes interference in the intense relationship between man and nature.

The refuge is built on a slope to take advantage of the thermal mass of the protecting hillside and to better fit into the surroundings.

The roof, finished in red tiles of a very similar colour to the local clays, rises at a counter angle from the slope, cutting an edge on the horizon of the plain when viewed from the highest part of the plot. Below this protecting surface stands the refuge, bonded to the ground by a clay floor (fired clay paving tiles), which extends outside towards a pool, next to the holm oak. On the north side the refuge is closed up and bounded by the solid box-like structure which contains a small bathroom, kitchen and fireplace. On the other sides it opens out generously so that the occupants can contemplate the sunset, in a composition set off by the water and the oak.

An atmosphere of abstraction is created by the use of only one material (fired clay), and the interior space is bathed in warm light which has an almost outside transparency in the living quarters and then fades to deep shadow in the sleeping area. Similarly, the method of construction also draws on the natural feel and simplicity of argillaceous materials. On a foundation of brick load-bearing walls, the exposed tees of rolled steel span overhangs and lintels in a touch of modernity. The rest of the materials, the ceramic board used as a base for the roof tiles, the fired clay paving tiles, the scratch coats texturized with an oxide patina, are undoubtedly timeless.

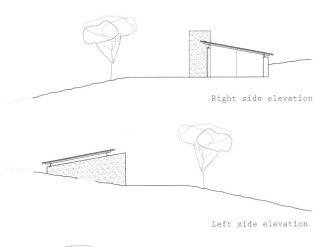

Right side elevation

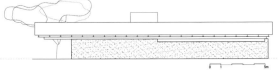

Left side elevation

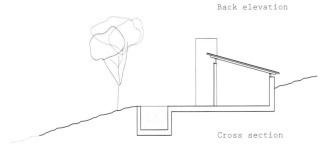

Back elevation

0 1 5m

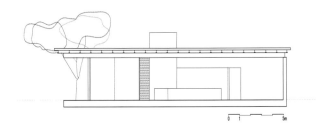

Cross section

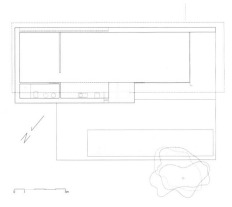

Long section

0 1 5m

Ground floor

0 1 5m

ARCHITECTS: Javier Bernalte and Jose Luis León
LOCATION: Paraje de la entresierra, Ciudad Real, Spain
DESIGN: 2001 **CONSTRUCTION:** 2001-2002 **DESIGN TEAM:** Javier
Bernalte and José Luis León with Rebeca Rubio **CLIENT:**
Catalina Cámara Díez **CONTRACTOR:** Rydemar **STRUCTURE AND
SERVICES ENGINEER:** Rydemar **PHOTOGRAPHER:** Ángel Baltanás

FLOOR TILE: fired clay paving tile
DIMENSIONS: 30 x 30 cm
ROOF TILE: unglazed clay tile, varnished with
colourless matt finish
DIMENSIONS: 70 x 30 cm

Restaurante Manduca
Madrid, Spain

The premises chosen for the Restaurante Manduca in Madrid are a generous space which structural renovation resolved on two levels. The premises were heavily partitioned due to the system of bearing walls that pertained, as a basic structure, to the 19th century structure of the ground floor. The tight budget for interior design accentuated the simplicity and lack of sophistication that the project was meant to highlight. From the entrance the layout of the spaces was such that the restaurant could be naturally arranged in a succession of dining rooms, providing diners with a choice of relatively intimate atmospheres.

Only three materials are used in the interior, all three natural and humble. The vertical planes are clad in the same bricks that are commonly used to erect partition walls in low-cost housing. These bricks, which are rendered, have a texture that is greatly enhanced by repetition and reflected light. The passages between the bearing walls are profiled with black varnished tiles, thus underscoring the transition that the thickness of these constructions, magnified by the superimposition of the ceramic material, supposes. The same tiles were used to redo the main staircase, which, in its original location, was slightly modified to simplify it and add value to its volumetric character within a higher space, at the underground level. Somewhat rough, black ceramic paving tiles, which partially cover a height of the walls, offer, along with the ceiling, a neutral background to underscore the lighting.

The linear lighting fitted behind the ceramic planes at the top and bottom of the walls reflects on the rough black surface of the ceiling and floor, lending the whole an ethereal, gauzy effect without obscuring the ceramic work. The rest of the lighting is designed to sustain as far as possible this somewhat mysterious effect, using floor lamps to intensify the beams of light on the tables without impacting on the main lighting.

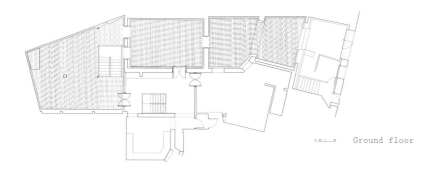

Ground floor

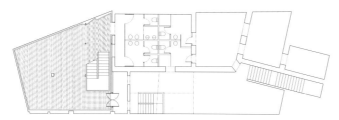

Basement floor

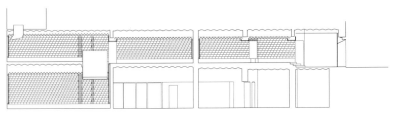

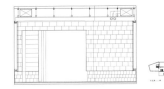

Section 1

Section of interior cladding

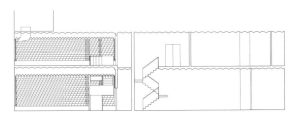

Section 2

ARCHITECT: Francisco Mangado **LOCATION:** c/ Sagasta 14,
Madrid, Spain **DESIGN:** 2002 **CONSTRUCTION:** 2003 **CLIENT:**
private **CONTRACTOR:** Later 2002 S.L. **STRUCTURAL ENGINEER:**
NB 35 S.L. **SERVICES ENGINEER:** Later 2002 S.L. **MECHANICAL
ENGINEER:** Iturralde y Sagues **PHOTOGRAPHER:** Roland Halbe

TILE: termoarcilla block (wall cladding)
DIMENSIONS: 30 x 19 x 5 cm

Processes for the product customization

Tiles can be modified to meet the needs of a project. These processes are usually performed after firing, though they may be done during pressing or in other pre-firing stages. These processes can be grouped according to the machinery used.

GRINDERS
Grinders, using a sintered diamond disc or wheel, are used to cut tiles to the desired size. Depending on the material, the grain of diamond and the binding agent may vary to achieve a clean cut. These machines are generally used to cut to size and square the edges of the piece; with porcelain they may be used to shape the edges.

HYDRAULIC CUTTERS
This technology uses a hydraulic circuit and pressure intensifier to subject water to high pressures (3000 to 4000 atm). The water is then directed through a diamond orifice approximately 0.2 mm in diameter to a mixing chamber where abrasive is added to bolster the cutting performance.

   The abrasive, generally garnet, is incorporated in the cutting jet by the Venturi effect produced by the water and then sent to the boron carbide or tungsten nozzle, 0.8 to 1.2 mm in diameter and some 7 cm long, where the abrasive acquires the speed and kinetic energy

1   Hydraulic cutter

2   Disc cutter

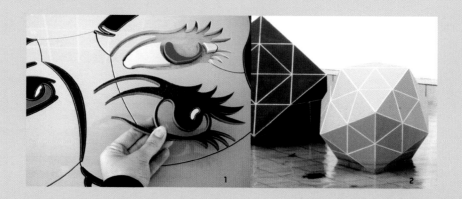

required to make the cut. The cutting speed depends on the material:
1 to 2 m/min. for single-fired tiles and stoneware, etc. and less
than 1 m/min. for porcelainic materials. For marble and granite,
depending on the thickness, it is difficult to get any better than
250m/min.

Although it is possible to make cuts a few millimetres wide,
it is very difficult to control the effects on the material to
achieve repeatability in the process. The system does, however,
offer absolute freedom in the direction of the jet.

DISC CUTTERS

As with grinders, these machines use sintered diamond discs some 300
to 350 mm in diameter and 1.2 to 2.4 mm thick, which are generally
mounted in rows in order to obtain a precise division of the piece
being cut.

This procedure is used to cut smaller pieces (listels, skirting,
etc.) from a larger one; it is a very common system and cuts all types
of ceramic materials, marble and granite. It cannot be used to cut
circles or to make cuts in the inner part of the tile.

Both grinders and disc cutters use water for cooling and
cleaning.

SAND BLASTERS

These machines spray sand at high pressures onto the piece. The areas
that are not meant to be affected are protected with an adhesive film.
The depth of the finishing is controlled by varying the time of application. The results are difficult to control dimensionally and the
application is manual.

3 Laser

LASER

As a tool for customizing tiles, the laser has a very promising
future, but it is still in the development stage and does not yet
have industrial applications.

Some of the future applications for this technology are:
- **Abrasion of the ceramic surface** It could be used for superficial
  treatments of unglazed materials such as porcelain; the effect
  achieved would be very similar to that of sand blasting, although
  the resolution and quality would be much better.
- **Modification of the subsurface glaze layer** It will be used on glazed
  pieces to change the chromatic value without affecting the surface
  texture.
- **Cutting of tiles** The laser will be used to cut ceramic pieces to
  any desired shape.

- **Customized graphic decoration** With the concentrated energy of the laser it is possible to fire a glaze selectively and thus create customized designs, even in situ and after the tiles have been fitted, using portable lasers.

PVD (PHYSICAL VAPOUR DEPOSITION)

PVD encompasses a series of coating technologies with which an extremely fine layer of material can be applied to ceramic pieces. The range of materials that can be used is very broad, including metals and alloys, which lend the tile their metallic appearance.

Given the fineness of the coating, the microstructure of the tile shows through, and thus, in the case of polished porcelain stoneware, for instance, the final product has the same shine as the original finish.

This technology is applicable to flat pieces as well as non-flat pieces and those with pronounced relief.

KERAJET

Kerajet uses ink-jet technology for decorating ceramic floor and wall tiles.

The system employs four basic colours of ink (cyan, magenta, yellow and black) and a digital image transfer process to decorate the piece with the desired motifs and shades. Since the ink is applied by means of jets, there is no direct contact with the tile. The system works for both flat tiles and those with relief or rounded edges.

Kerajet achieves speeds ranging from 10m/min. (minimum speed) to a maximum of 50m/min. Another variable to bear in mind is the setting of the heads, which must be adjusted according to the thickness of the tile: the closer the heads are to the surface of the tile, the better the results.

The advantages of this decorating system are the no-touch printing, speed and excellent control. Moreover, the entire process is digital, so that changes can be made easily without the need for new inks or stencils.

THE FOLDING OF TILES

The system consists of putting the tiles on a mould and heating them in a roller kiln until they acquire plasticity, at which point they fold and adopt the form of the mould.

In order to ensure that the tile folds at the right points, a series of precisely measured incisions must be made in it. The system is used for making steps, corner pieces, gutters, skirting, etc.

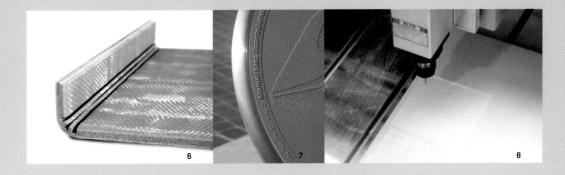

6   7   8

ACQUIRING AND MILLING OF RELIEFS

Tile manufacturers use special machinery to add relief to their tiles. These machines normally use laser readers and thus there is no contact between the surface to read and the pick-up device, which means that they can acquire reliefs and textures from a large number of sources, among them non-cohesive minerals and organic materials.

Once the surface has been acquired or directly computer-generated, it can be applied to a range of materials with numerically controlled milling machines. Depending on what the prototype is to be used for, one material or another will be used in the process. If we want the product to be perfectly functional with an acceptable production run (roughly 3,000 units), we need a material that will withstand that much wear and not lose detail in the pressing, for which teflon or hard resins are used. Should a greater number of pieces be required, a heated die is used.

JAVIER MIRA PEIDRO is a technical architect (Polytechnic University of Valencia). He has been a member ALICER since its founding in April 1993. Currently he is the Association's vice director and directs its Architecture Department.
He is coordinator of nine ceramic tile R+D projects, related to design, architectural applications and innovative decorative processes.
He has published several articles published in scientific or technical journals and the specialized press for the sector.
He has given numerous conferences at several congresses.
He has won four prizes for his projects from Spanish and international design competitions.

Interaction

We might say that our education as architects has always been informed by the urge to engage in materials research in order to carry out our projects. Drawing on both innovation and tradition, we use these materials to experiment with textures, forms and colours (**1, 2, 3**). These are periods of intense activity, in which in our hands the manipulation and modification of the material becomes a sort of game. We might define this process as an exercise in material skills (**4, 5**).

We consider that the most important part of this process is when we get together with the manufacturer to trade opinions and decide how best to deal with the material in order to produce the ideal model. This process also entails major changes both in the design and in the application of the material in the building. Experts in the field lend certain viability, in real terms of manufacturing and application to our research.

One of our first jobs as architects was a research study into dry-fitted small-size ceramic tile. Our success in that endeavour was largely thanks to our continuous communication with the manufacturer, who gave us access to a wealth of information which proved necessary for the development of the system (**6**). The terminology of ceramics manufacturing — pressing, extrusion, casting, drying, firing, absorption, glazing — has become part of our vocabulary. These are key words the architect must be conversant with in order to understand ceramics production systems, the properties of the product, its size, colours and textures; they are basic parameters which enable one to start thinking in terms of ceramics.

On the other hand, it is essential to define the rules of play and arrive at an equilibrium between manufacturer and architect to facilitate a professional relationship that enables each side to contribute the best they have to offer. This point of equilibrium is achieved in the joining of different disciplines, technologies and fields of expertise and action, generating a state of exchange — of transversality — that facilitates progress and synergy with the material itself. We understand that rather than from the simple idea of innovation, this emerges from an attitude of sensitivity towards the material. It is a matter of generating a receptive attitude which produces an open process of investigation. Innovation is the result of continuity and the way in which a business (industry) and a professional (architect) join forces in a project and foment its development. A need exists for interaction between architect and manufacturer in the realm of innovation of ceramic materials, an interaction that we must promote and feed off of to raise the profile of ceramics in architecture today.

Clear examples of interaction between manufacturer and architect that have engendered new ways of understanding ceramics with highly significant results are found in works of contemporary architecture, such as: Santa Caterina Market and Parque Diagonal Mar by Enric Miralles and Benedetta Tagliabue; Peñíscola Congress Centre by Paredes Pedrosa arquitectos; The Casa Barcelona 2005 project by Vicente Sarrablo; The Ircam building in Paris and the Cité Universitaire in Lyon by Renzo Piano.

1 and 2 Concrete and plaster pieces moulded with a shuttering made out of reeds. The goal was to achieve this texture on the main walls of the project.

3 Concrete piece moulded with a shuttering made out of reeds. Model designed to be used as a system for making slabs.

4 and 5 Study for paving tiles. In reference to the place of action, we defined a ceramic paving that comprised a set of 7 different pieces that fitted together, and that reproduced "x" times on the same plane recalled cracked earth.

6 Research project for the development of a ceramic cladding system for ventilated façades.

JORDI ROVIRAS MIÑANA and CRISTINA GARCÍA CASTELAO Architects dedicated primarily to building, teaching and research. Tutors of the Construction Department at School of Architecture of the International University of Catalonia. Tutors in the discretionary credit course of the Chair of Ceramic Studies at School of Architecture of the International University of Catalonia.

Congress Centre
Peñíscola, Spain

The project was defined to a large extent by the location of the Congress Centre, below Peñíscola Castle and opposite a garden behind the Mediterranean seafront.

From the surrounding streets, the building appears continuous and closed while from the garden it looks fragmented and open, with a large plaza to allow the future park to penetrate to the doors. Meanwhile, the interior spaces are orientated towards the park and sea (seen from the upper floor).

A latticework, providing the transition between the park and the interior space, is the architectural element that materializes both this accord and the image of the future Centre. It is made of ceramic pieces hung from a lightweight metal bar-and-bracket structure, forming a three-dimensional fabric. This structure, providing at once interior and exterior space, permeable to the air but sheltered from the rain, is the building's anteroom, a meeting point before the lobby, slipped in between the volumes of white reinforced concrete.

The building's fourth façade is the roof, visible from the Castle, with the undulating slab of reinforced concrete covering the main hall clad in zinc.

The lobby is designed as a fluid and enveloping interior at the centre of the different parts of the building arrayed round it like autonomous pieces. The ground floor includes the access to the hall, administrative offices and exhibition hall, at a slightly lower level than the lobby. On the first floor, surrounding this inner void, are arranged the congress halls, pressroom and café, opening visually onto the park and with a large 'eye' providing views of the sea.

The main hall, with seating capacity for 702 people on one continuous gently sloping plane, is designed for concerts, congresses and screenings. The roof is an undulating slab of bare reinforced concrete, the structure of which meets the acoustic requirements of the space. The walls are clad in mobila timber planks, which cover the lateral technical galleries and provide the vertical counterpoint to the bare white reinforced concrete ceiling.

In addition to the bare white structural reinforced concrete and mobila timber panelling, the other materials seen in the interior of the building are grey slate on the floors and the fine metal structure on the ceilings, which incorporates the hidden and continuous light fixtures and other fittings.

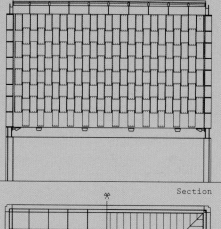
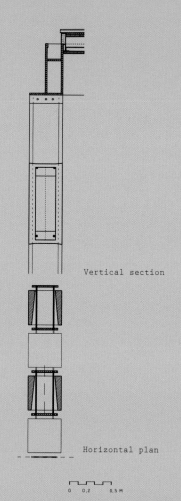

Elevation

Section

Vertical section

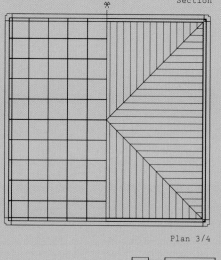

Plan 1/2

Plan 3/4

Horizontal plan

```
0   2      5
```
Access atrium

```
0  0,2   0,5 M
```

The ceramic pieces of the latticework recall the three-dimensional ceramic elements used in traditional architecture and the Modern Movement of the 20th century.

The ceramic tiles which cover the entrance to the Centre, with the criterion of a large facility, recall, however, the character — of open space perforated by the sun and air, of transitional space, cool and shaded during the day and magical at night — that the ceramic latticework has always provided.

A total of 400 (in reality, a few more, since the moulding and firing research process proved more difficult than expected) natural texture stoneware pieces, 100 x 40 x 40 cm and weighing some 80 kg each, were manufactured, fired at high temperature.

Unexpected problems cropped up. The large manufacturers refused to interrupt work to embark on a venture whose outcome was unknown, and the pieces were made manually by Valencian artisans who had even more reservations than the architects. With contemporary firing techniques, the first pieces deformed beyond what was admissible and, because of the large volume of water they had to lose, a gradual firing, such as that obtained in old kilns, was deemed necessary.

In the same way that we had set out in search of tile-makers, we went on a new quest for kilns, in the face of an efficient and incredulous builder, and swimming against the tide of standard industrial procedure and time-saving measures. The pieces were tested, of course, with modern quality control methods and the results showed surprising strength for both the dry and wet piece.

The natural ceramic tone was achieved by moderating the firing temperature and the pieces were fitted to a lightweight metal rod-and-bracket structure at the entrance to the Centre.

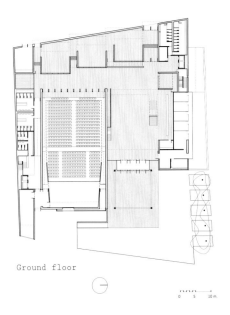

Ground floor

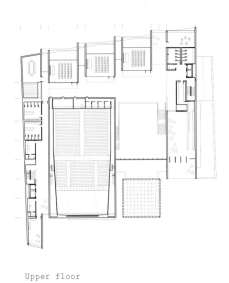

Upper floor

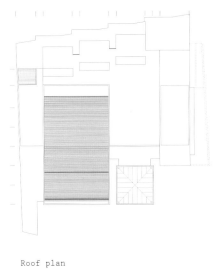

Roof plan

0 5 10 m.

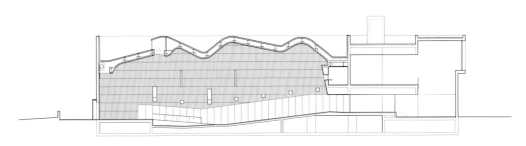

Main hall long section

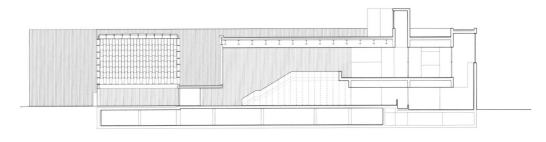

Lobby long section

ARCHITECTS: Paredes Pedrosa arquitectos **LOCATION:**
c/ Maestro Bayarri, c/ Blasco Ibáñez, 12598
Peñíscola, Spain **DESIGN:** 2001 (competition 2000)
CONSTRUCTION: 2002-2003 **DESIGN TEAM:** Ignacio García
Pedrosa and Ángela García de Paredes with Eva M.
Neila, Silvia Colmenares, Javier Arpa
SITE ASSOCIATES: Jaime Prior, Ramón Monfort **CONSTRUCTION
SURVEYOR:** Luis Calvo, José Carratalá **CLIENT:** Proyecto
Cultural de Castellón, S.A. **CONTRACTOR:** COMSA
STRUCTURAL ENGINEER: Gogaite S.L. **SERVICES ENGINEER:** EPM
S.L., AXIMA S.A. **PHOTOGRAPHERS:** Roland Halbe (p88,
89, 91), Lluís Casals (p92)

TILE DESIGN: Ángela García de Paredes, Ignacio García
Pedrosa and Vicente Díez
TILE PIECES: stoneware
PRODUCT DIMENSIONS: 100 x 40 x 40 cm

Ceramic tile and modern technological levity

If we were to ask ourselves which material represents modernity in architecture it is hardly likely that ceramic tile would come to mind. The image of the Modern Movement, as an international style, is forged in 1931 with the book by Johnson and Hitchcock: smooth white prisms, great squashed perforations, large spans of glass in metal frames. This is an architecture that sees itself in technology and recreates in novel nautical style the objectivity of the engineer and big industry, that of a lightweight, precise and clean construction of metal panels and laminated glass.

But, examined crosswise, the figuration of this brief period of avant-garde reveals a much richer modernity. Few movements have been more multiform, given that its unifying principle, spiritual sincerity — the rejection of historicist imposture, of the superficiality of purely personal taste — is non-figurative. Thus, in Germany, the Expressionist Movement, as F. Höger shows in his Chile-Haus (1923) or Behrens shows in the Höchster office building (1920-24), finds in ceramics the material with which to build a vibrant architecture without relying on applied ornamentation. And, in Holland, Dudok and de Klerk defend as part of objectivity leaving bare the bricks with which they erect their works.

Given this diversity, as well as the versatility of the material itself, it would be a long, arduous endeavour to give a complete picture of the use of ceramics in modern architecture. Thus, by way of an approach, we shall examine the architectures of the great masters (Le Corbusier, Mies van der Rohe and Aalto) to see how its use was reinvented (structure, ribbing and cladding) over the course of the 20th century.

Le Corbusier is the prime representative of modernity as an avant-garde, especially in his architecture from the twenties, and the white perfection of his houses from this early period speak more of technological aspiration than of any reality. The exact prisms conceal an ordinary construction, and the ceramic materials, material from a bygone era, are hidden. He moves beyond this purist ideality in the thirties, with the recognition of the complexity of what is real. Thus, the rubble walls of the Week-end house in La Celle Saint-Cloud (1935) or the brickwork on the Jaoul houses (1952-56) are exposed for what they are. But the technological novelty that remains foremost in Le Corbusier's mind is reinforced concrete. And his walls, whether of rubble or brick, are always conceived as a mass whose component parts have no individuality. Each piece, whether irregular or geometrically precise, vanishes within the general abstract pattern, emerging only as texture. In the Sarabhai house (1955), the lines that define the bays through which the spaces flow are materialized on two different levels, ceramic material and reinforced concrete, depending on their structural function, which introduces variety in colours and textures: nonetheless they are part of a single conceptual plan.

The modern ideality of Mies is not so technological as it is spiritual, despite the appearances of his latter works, and is closely linked with the German Expressionist scene of his youth. In one of his first modern projects, the brick house (1923), in contrast to the structural preoccupation of the reinforced concrete house (1924), the thick lines centre only on the spatial and compositional exploration. It seems similar to the rationalized Expressionism of De Stijl, but as in the monument to Rosa Luxemburg (1926), the abstract geometry is brought to life by the concretion of the forthright ceramic texture.

When redrawing this same house, probably by then in the US, each of the bricks that comprise the walls is defined. They are afforded the same individuality as the sections of the marble cladding on the Barcelona Pavilion (1928-29). They make up a whole in which each of the pieces is regarded as a perfect element: from the mass, in a generic technology, to a joining of pieces, in a specific technology.

Where this process becomes most evident is in the IIT campus buildings (1938-58). The structure is a metalwork web that, due to technological imperatives and in contrast with the first projects, does not the set back the columns but rather locates them flush with the façade. Thus, the ceramic work, necessarily fill-in, is treated like a panel, like something that is inserted. Like the carpentery work, it might have been manufactured at the factory and then fitted on site. This reading is what the details offer, the joining that clearly delimits the perimeter and frees it from the structural framework.

But this seeming technological novelty is no such thing: it had originated in Chicago, in answer to the need to cover metals structures with lightweight, fireproof elements. In the works of Sullivan, terracotta, thanks to its plasticity, serves his architectural theory in the ornamental unity that runs unbroken over the entire building from base to cornice. The singularity of Mies lies in introducing spiritual sincerity into the technology, in exposing the application of the ceramics. And this is what Renzo Piano would take to its highest expression, on the façade of the IRCAM (1988-90), by suspending within a metal framework each of the ceramic pieces that comprise the panel. The pieces appear individually, with open joints, for each one bears only its own weight.

95

1   Seinajoki Town Hall (1961-1965) by Alvar Aalto. Photographer: Simo Rista.

2   House of Culture, Helsinki (1955-58) by Alvar Aalto. Photographer: Rauno Träskelin

3   Metallurgical and Chemical Engineering Building (ITT), Chicago (1945) by Ludwig Mies van der Rohe. Photographer: Yukio Futagawa

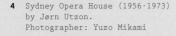

4 Sydney Opera House (1956-1973)
by Jørn Utzon.
Photographer: Yuzo Mikami

5 Sydney Opera House (1956-1973)
by Jørn Utzon.
Photographer: Max Dupain

Aalto, unlike Mies, does not start from Expressionism to then
avail himself of technology in order to empty it of all but its
spirituality. His first modern works almost coincide with the early
thirties, with the realist critique of the technological utopia, and
the acceptance of the surrealist influence. The expression is not
so much the fruit of the individual artist as it is of the collective
unconscious, of the acceptance of the raw materials of tradition
and of their contrast with modern technological elements. And the
sincerity is also analogy, and it avoids the inconsistency of
affirming contemporaneousness through an unnecessary visual deployment
of technology.

We might speculate on the influence of the Nordic vernacular
tradition, of the timber constructions whose total covering conceals
the structure, and where each element maintains an individuality that
manifests itself in a tectonically textured whole. The fact is that
those elements that originally appear discreetly inside Rationalist
buildings, for example, the ceramic pipe lattice of the exhibition
pavilions (1937-39), end up encompassing the totality. The rich

6 Girasol Building. Madrid
   (1966) by José Antonio
   Coderch.
   Photographer: F. Català-Roca

7 French Institute. Barcelona
   (1972) by José Antonio
   Coderch.
   Photographer: F. Català-Roca

texture offered by the diversity of brick patterns in the courtyard
of his summer home (1953) is an early, timid demonstration of what,
in subsequent buildings, assumes openly the role of cladding, both in
interiors — the fasciculated effect of the glazed ceramic half pipes
covering the central parts of the columns — and in exteriors, on the
Seinajoki Town Hall (1961-65).

   Glazed ceramic tiles have been accepted by modern architecture.
Their capacity to reflect and create a vibrant surface lends them
a life of their own, mobile and lightweight. In the Barcelona
Tuberculosis Sanatorium (1934-36), by Sert, Torres Clavé and Subirana,
they clad those partitions to lend them etherealness, to express the
continuity of the space under the piloti. This is what Coderch
resorted to in his flat block in Barceloneta (1951), where large
stretches of the façade are also covered in glazed tiles, showing
themselves to be as light as the shutters that accompany them. And in
the French Institute (1972) or, more so, in the Girasol Building
(1966) the ceramic panels are arranged in vertical courses, so as to
imply that the enclosure is a fine layer without weight-bearing
capacity, and it dangles below the first-floor slab, to show just
how flimsy it is. But it is Utzon, in his Sydney Opera House (1957),
who makes a more forthright use of this capacity. The forms that he
had imagined as fine shells of reinforced concrete were eventually
built as a series of thick voussoirs covered in glazed ceramic plates,
the shade of Chinese porcelain, to achieve the original lightness,
the ideal technological levity of modern architecture.

RAFAEL DIEZ BARREÑADA (Barcelona, 1964) Architect and associate tutor at the Projects
Department of the ETSAB. His writings on modern architecture include the book *Coderch.
Variaciones sobre una casa*. Fundación Caja de Arquitectos, 2003, and the monographic issue
dedicated to José Antonio Coderch of the journal 2G (no. 33, 2005).

La Ricarda
El Prat del Llobregat, Spain

In 1953 Bonet presented a project for a summer and weekend residence which would not be completed until 1963 after a lengthy construction process. The basic characteristics are a recurring structural module consisting of a vault (8,80 x 8,80 m) supported by metal columns, and a series of materials which compose the enclosing planes. Thus, distinct interactions with the surrounding landscape are defined using the following devices: transparent glass, tile latticework, tile latticework with translucent glass inserts, walls clad with ceramics, planes of slats made up of timber roller blinds.

The building is laid out as the cruciform intersection of two units: the north-south unit accommodates, under a barrel vault, the six bedrooms set out in pairs, while the east-west unit accommodates the livingroom, dining room and kit-chen complex under four successive vaults. Two other features complete the house: on the east side there is an auxiliary pavilion for the caretakers and a garage oriented north-south, which terminates the "entrance courtyard", and there is an "independent pavilion" situated to the west, a unit that contains the parents' bedroom. It is secluded but, at the same time, connected to the rest of the house by an almost invisible corridor. The front entrance is situated where the two main units intersect. What made La Ricarda an innovative design was the cruciform intersection of this series of units with the idea of establishing a strict arrangement as a device for the regulation and layout of the interior and exterior spaces.

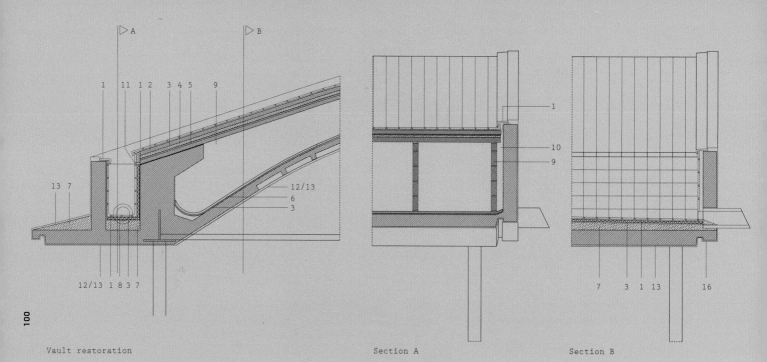

Section A

Section B

Vault restoration

1 "cucurny" ferruginous stoneware tile and trimmer 12 x 12 x 1.5 cm
fixed with elastic or asphalt mortar
2 4/5 cm underlay with 30 # and Ø3 mesh
3 waterproof membrane
4 levelling screed
5 ceramic sheathing
6 3 cm underlay with 30 # and Ø3 mesh
7 formation of inclines with perlite mortar
8 insulation with 2 cm thick layer of expanded polystyrene
9 brick supporting wall, 50 x 25 x 4 cm
10 extruded polyurethane
11 expansion joint
12 plaster finish
13 lime plaster stucco
14 structural concrete 250kg/cm2
15 "curcurny" stoneware scupper
16 10 cm thick structural vault

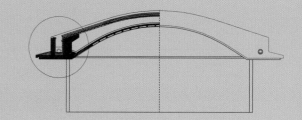

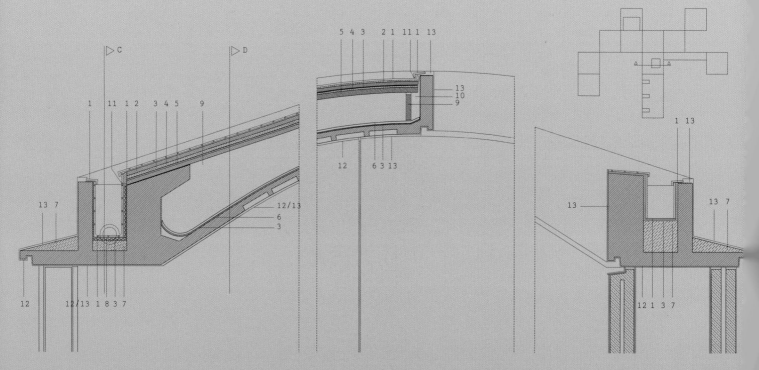

Section C

Section D

During the execution of the air cavities, supporting ribs were erected to hold up the ceramic sheathing.

The structural vault was insulated with a 60 mm layer of polyurethane foam.

The exterior vault and gutters were sealed with a waterproof membrane, which was protected by a layer of mortar with a light reinforcement.

When the stoneware pieces were fixed on the surface prepared to this effect, expansion joints were incorporated at the ends, by the gutters and flashing.

More than a dozen tests were made to find a type of stoneware which matched the colour, patina and texture of the original pieces which had been conserved.

The restoration The Ricarda house has been undergoing restoration since 1997. In order to draw up a plan for the restoration it was decided to carry out detailed surveys to diagnose the condition of the house. The first survey dealt exclusively with the roof vaults and included an analysis of coverings, waterproofing, insulation, ventilation of air cavities, drainage, repair of the underlying structure, etc. The second survey tackled the foundations the structure, coverings, flooring, installations and services, and other furnishings and fittings.

The vaults When drawing up the project for their restoration, a survey was made of the vaults to analyse their geometry and the details of their system of construction: individual reinforced concrete lintels, metal supporting structure, reinforced concrete beams, reinforced concrete vault braced with various profiles and lightened with an interstitial filling of 9 cm thick hollow bricks, air cavity and ventilation, thermal insulation, roof vault on supporting walls, damp courses, cladding, rendering, plasterwork, etc. The main difficulty on dealing with this complex design consisted of identifying and prioritising the problems to be solved on the basis of the visible damage that spoilt the appearance of the house: flaking stucco, cracked or broken tiles on the roofs, damp patches and leaks due to waterproofing in poor conditions, interior condensation, rusting and peeling on metal structures, worn and ageing varnish and paint finishes.

The restoration was conditioned by the unobtainability of some materials from the construction market of the seventies, such as the 12 x 12 salt-glazed stoneware manufactured by the Cucurny company — no longer trading — which cladded the vaults: identical pieces had to be manufactured in the workshops of Toni Cumella. Three areas in the vaults were studied to determine the colour, shade and sheen, and a series of tests were made to determine the definitive aspect of the pieces.

During the project the details of tile joints were also studied, and the expansion joints between the exterior vault and its perimeter, between distinct coverings of stoneware and between the stoneware cladding itself and the final stucco were determined to avoid future cracking — one of the most noticeable and predictable problems. The restoration of the vaults was completed between June 1999 and June 2000.

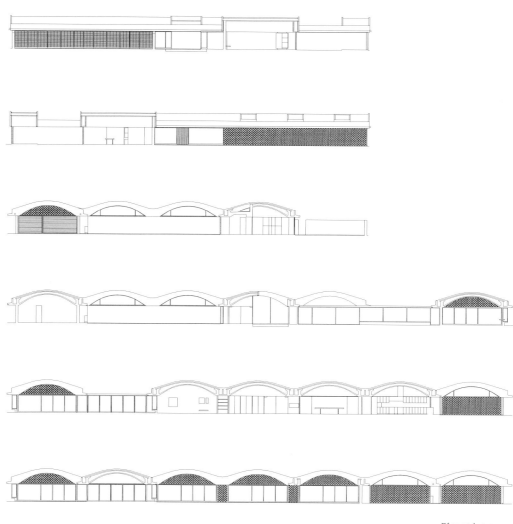

Elevations

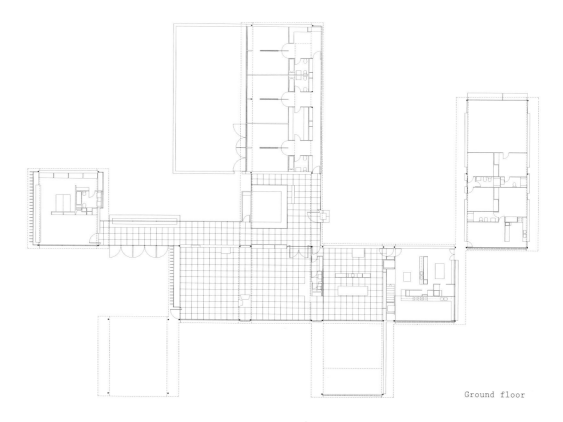

Ground floor

ARCHITECT: Antonio Bonet Castellana LOCATION: Residence
La Ricarda, El Prat del Llobregat, Spain DESIGN: 1953
CONSTRUCTION: 1962 CONSTRUCTION SURVEYOR: José Comas CLIENT:
Ricardo Gomis e Inés Bertrand CONTRACTOR AND CONSTRUCTION
SURVEYOR: Emilio Bofill (on the suggestion of Antonio
Bonet) RESTORATION ARCHITECTS: Fernando Alvarez Prozorovich
and Jordi Roig Navarro (restoration) RESTORATION: 1997-
2004 RESTORATION DESIGN TEAM: Fernando Álvarez and Jordi
Roig with Heiko Trittler, Carlos Casablancas, Felix
López, Carlos Bermudez, Salvador Auge RESTORATION
CONTRACTOR: Zurriaga PHOTOGRAPHERS: Jordi Bernadó (p98,
99, 103), Fernando Álvarez and Jordi Roig (building
site in progress)

TILE: salt-glazed stoneware
DIMENSIONS: 12 x 12 x 1,5 cm

Parque Diagonal Mar
Barcelona, Spain

Parque Diagonal Mar is a large park that stretches as far as the adjacent avenues. Its design and location make it one of the most extensive of Barcelona's great gardens, because it is connected to the Avenida Diagonal, Taulat and, in particular, directly to the beach.

The very design of the park helps it to blend into the surrounding cityscape. It is laid out on the basis of a series of paths which branch away in all directions like a tree. The main part of the park, a kind of "rambla", or boulevard, links the Diagonal directly to the nearby beach, crossing the ring road via a pedestrian bridge.

This main path is broken up into a series of lanes for skaters and cyclists, and runs alongside the edge of a large lake which, together with the areas planted with trees, is what gives the park its character. It is from this lake that the park is best viewed. The lake is a sizeable expanse of water with a waterfall and vegetation growing along the edges to aerate the water. It is a place for recreation, with boating, fountains, children's play area and so on.

Vegetation typical of salt marshes grows near the sea and around the lake. It becomes progressively taller and denser further away from the lake and extends as far as the streets that border the park. Where the vegetation and the paths meet at the edges of the park they form a series of spaces like small squares.

A series of large ceramic urns stand or hang in these spaces and blend in with the existing vegetation. The effect is reminiscent of a private garden with benches, pergolas, etc.

Floor plan of Parque de Diagonal Mar

ARCHITECTS: EMBT Arquitectes LOCATION: Diagonal Mar,
Barcelona, Spain DESIGN: 1997 CONSTRUCTION: 2002
DESIGN TEAM: Enric Miralles and Benedetta Tagliabue
with Fabián Asunción, Lluis Cantallops, Elena Rocchi
(project director) and Mònica Batalla, Angelo Catania,
Ezequiel Cattaneo, Massimo Chizzola, Piercarlo
Comacchio, Stefan Eckert, Michael Eichhorn, Angelo
Floros, Makoto Fukuda, Makoto Fukuda, Stefan Geenen,
Jan Marko Grebe, Wolfang Lukas, Hainz, Christine
Himmler, Cristofer Hofler, Hirotaka Koizumi, Georg
Mahnke, Andrea Möller, Dani Rosselló, Kaori Sato,
Roberto Sforza, Ulrike Stübner, Francesca Tata,
Laura Valentini, Adrian Versuere MODEL: Riccardo
Alessandroni, Fabián Asuncion, Tobias Aus Der

Beek, Charlotte Bojsen-Möller, Liliana Bonforte,
Vazquez Mónica Carrera Vazquez, Sven Gosmann, Tobias
Gottschalk, Adria Goula Francesco Jacques-Dias, Jan
Koettgen, Pierre Lauper, Andrea Möller, Isabelle
Sambeth, Luca Tonella, Isabel Zaragoza DEVELOPER:
Diagonal Mar/Hines CONTRACTOR: Benjumea LANDSCAPE
ARCHITECTS: Edaw, Londres URBAN DESIGN: Oscar Tusquets,
Xavier Sust STRUCTURAL AND SERVICES ENGINEER: Europroject
Consultores Asociados, José María Velasco (engineer)
PHOTOGRAPHER: Toni Cumella

TILE: glazed and serigraphed white stoneware
DIMENSIONS: 10 types with different designs and in
varying sizes (from 10 x 5 cm to 40 x 30 cm)

Award-winner in the 3rd Edition of Tile of Spain
Awards of Architecture and Interior Design (2004-2005)

Restoration of the Santa Caterina Market
Barcelona, Spain

The Santa Caterina market is one of the oldest markets in Barcelona and was built before the demolition of the city walls around 1848. The building owes its name to the old Gothic convent of Santa Caterina, which dated from the 13th century. After the destruction of the convent the market was built over the remains, though the apse of the church is still partially conserved. It is situated on the corner of the streets, calle Colomines and calle Giralt el Pellicer, and can be visited since the restoration of the market.

A description of project does not tally with the typical concept of restoration, but because of the limitations imposed by the conservation of façades it cannot be said to be a new building.

The project deals with three operative strategies:

1. To challenge the dichotomy between old and new, by acknowledging that the original structure that has lasted up to the present day is up-to-date, useful and contemporary.

2. To defend the idea of use and reuse, as opposed to demolition. The new constructions are superimposed on the existing ones, interacting and blending in to highlight the finer qualities of the structure. Thus, the project may be described in terms such as conglomerate or hybrid.

3. The play on disparity as a way of acknowledging the superimposition of elements from different periods. The constant variations are fruit of the idea of repetition and renewal, to ensure that the project is not focussed or anchored in one particular period of time.

The project starts out by reviewing the existing layout and proposes a model adapted to the complexity of the site, by means of a design where it is not easy to distinguish between restoration and new structures.

On a practical level, the modification of the market contemplates the creation of areas designated for diverse uses at variance with the main function of the market. Below ground level these areas include the pneumatic refuse collection plant on the lowest floor (level -3), which serves the Barcelona district of Ciutat Vella, the two floors of parking space for saloon cars, an area for supplying the market, and a zone reserved for visits to the apse of the old convent church. The market stalls, a library, an access to the remains of the apse, a supermarket and loading bays for lorries and vans which supply the market are located on the ground floor, and there is a five-storey residential block at the rear.

The project rationalises the distribution of accesses and services, displaces the commercial area towards Avenida Cambó, reducing its scale, and opens up the old structure of the market towards the interior of the Santa Caterina neighbourhood. In addition, the project provides public space and housing.

From the standpoint of construction, the project provides coherent solutions in line with the strategies drawn up in the master plan. The undulating roof is the feature which most clearly reflects the structural complexity of the design in a constant play on superimposition and perspective. This construction combines post-tensioned concrete, metal structures and timber; it is clad with polychromatic ceramic pieces designed in collaboration with the ceramicist Toni Cumella.

Market floor

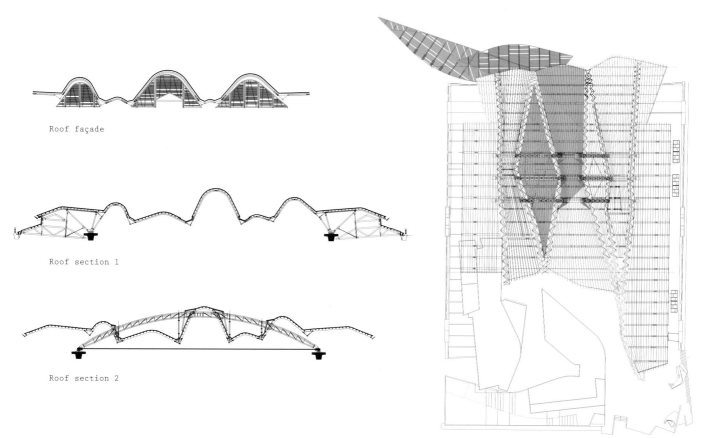

Roof façade

Roof section 1

Roof section 2

Upper floor

ARCHITECTS: EMBT Arquitectes LOCATION: av/ Cambó s/n, Barcelona, Spain COMPETITION: 1997 COMPLETION: 2005 DESIGN TEAM: Enric Miralles and Benedetta Tagliabue with Igor Peraza (project leader), Barbara Appolloni, Fabian Asunción, Sabine Bauchmann, Nils Becker, Josep Belles, Liliana Bonforte, Alicia Bramon, Joan Callis, Lluis Cantallops, Monica Carrera, Jorge Carvajal, Marta Cases, Constanza Chara, Marco Dario Chirdel, Massimo Chizzola, Eugenio Cirulli, Lluis Corbella, Santiago Crespi, Ane Ebbeskov Olsen, Stefan Eckert, Ricardo Flores, Marc Forteza Parera, Makoto Fukuda, Montse Galindo, Anna Galmer, Stefan Geenen, Loïc Gestin, Leonardo Giovannozzi, Tobias Gottschalk, Ute Grölz, Gianfranco Grondona, Fernanda Hannah, Annie Marcela Henao, Ezequiel Cattaneo, Annette Hoëller, Francesco Jacques-Dias, Hirotaka Kuizumi, Andrea Landell de Moura, Stephanie Le Draoullec, Josep Miàs, Christian Molina, Raphael de Montard, Francesco Mozzati, Peter Sándor Nagy, Barbara Oel Brandt, Mette Olsen, Adelaide Passetti, Joan Poca, Eva Prats, Ignacio Quintana, Elena Rocchi, Dani Rosselló, Torsten Schmid, Torsten Skoetz, Silke Techen, Luca Tonella, Anna Maria Tosi, Karl Unglaub, Laura Valentini, Jean François Vaudeville, Alejandra Vazquez, Maarten Vermeiren, Adrien Verschuere, Florencia Vetcher, Thomas Wuttke, German Zambrana CLIENT: Foment de Ciutat Vella S.A. CONTRACTOR: COMSA STRUCTURAL ENGINEER: Robert Brufau SERVICES ENGINEER: PGI ROOFING ENGINEER: Jose Maria Velasco HOUSING ENGINEER: Miquel Llorens PHOTOGRAPHERS: Duccio Malagamba (p109, 111, 112, 113), Toni Cumella, the architects (tiles in workshop)

TILE: glazed white stoneware in 67 colours fired at high temperature
DIMENSIONS: 2,000 regular hexagonal pieces, 15 cm wide

Award-winner in the 3rd Edition of Tile of Spain Awards of Architecture and Interior Design (2004-2005)

Spanish Pavilion, Expo 2005
Aichi, Japan

One of the most critical questions that needs addressing in the early 21st century by the international community — the main participant in an international exhibition — is how to foment a more productive relationship between Western and Middle Eastern cultures. On this occasion, in a country which represents a third culture, that of an Asian society, it seems fitting to reaffirm, through the architectural characteristics of this pavilion, the synthesis between Islamic and Judeo-Christian cultures that occurred in the Iberian Peninsula during several centuries and which forms a crucial part of Spanish cultural tradition. We consider that a pavilion designed to represent a country should try to link its history and traditions to a vision of the future. Therefore, by way of a general strategy to articulate this proposition, we reviewed historical models, both architectural and figurative, and their adaptation and modernisation to create new ones.

The pavilion is organised around a large, central zone, an empty space which links up the rest of the building and serves as an antechamber. This empty space connects on one side to the Romanesque and Gothic naves, characterised by their predominant verticality and a monumentalist effect achieved by the sheer disproportion between the space and the visitors. The church nave gives on to the chapels, where the more specific "contents" are concentrated: the "treasures", the exhibitions. In contrast to this model of church nave, we reverted to the typology — and layout — of the courtyard, another archetype with Mediterranean and Middle-Eastern origins, where an outside space on a much more intimate scale coordinates the structure of the household. Essentially, the Nave or Courtyard forms the central and vertical space, while the exterior space is arranged so that it functions as a sort of abstract enclosure and may be used for multiple purposes.

A series of small rooms are distributed round around the nave-courtyard, in a sharp reduction in scale. The same as in the cathedral chapels, hermitages, sanctuaries or the rooms in sequence which structure family life in a Muslim home, these are welcoming intimates areas, where the visitors' attention is drawn to the artefacts, the iconic exhibits, for their direct appreciation. This contraction/expansion of the space works extremely well as an exhibitionistic resource. It is a surprise factor that shifts levels of attention and interest and gives an area of limited dimensions greater spatial variety.

Ceramic element: fixing detail

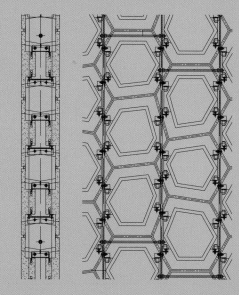

Ceramic element: section and elevations

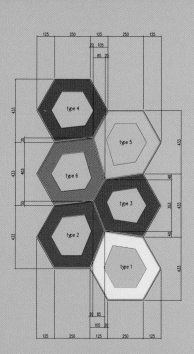

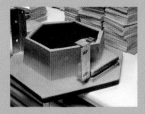

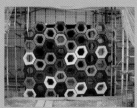

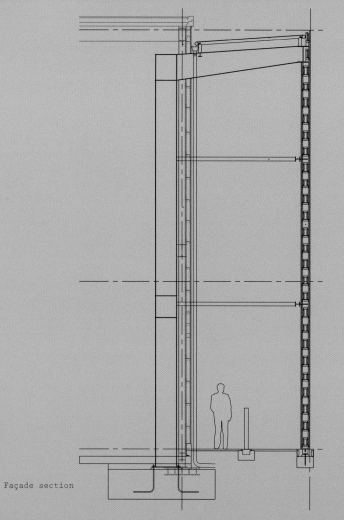

Façade section

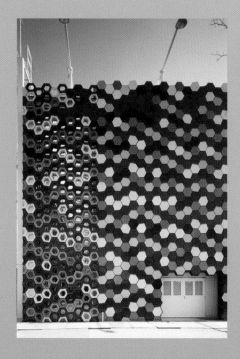

The façade Instead of representing something iconic we decided to resort to a lattice, a popular element in Spanish architecture. It consists in a large perforated wall surrounds the pavilion at a distance of 1.5 m, thus leaving an interstitial space that acts as a porch. This is an area of transition between the interior and the exterior, a place that filters the light and provides shelter, ideal to accommodate the queues of visitors waiting to enter the pavilion. This kind of space is also found in traditional Japanese architecture, in the temples of Kyoto for example, where the limit between the interior and the exterior is blurred by a number of membranes.

The traditional geometric arrangements are created by aggregating regular figures which normally form a pattern on a larger scale. The challenge was to come up with an irregular arrangement that produces a homogeneous but constantly varying pattern. We achieved this by using seven distinct hexagonal pieces, whose size depends on their system of production.

The pieces are **ceramic material**, a basic element in traditional and contemporary Spanish architecture. The trouble taken to produce them in Spain and transport them to Nagoya is offset by the impact produced by bringing over "Spanish earth", by putting the visitor in close contact with a part of Spanish land and Spanish culture. In addition, Aichi is well known in Japan for its tradition in ceramics, another reason why the material is a meeting-point between the Spanish and Japanese cultures.

Given the distinctiveness of the pieces the best way of recycling them would be symbolic: they could be donated as children's games to nursery schools in Nagoya, or be set up in parks as sculptures, so that the earth of Spain would become part of Japan at the end of the Expo.

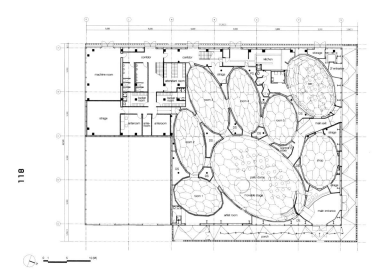

Ground floor plan

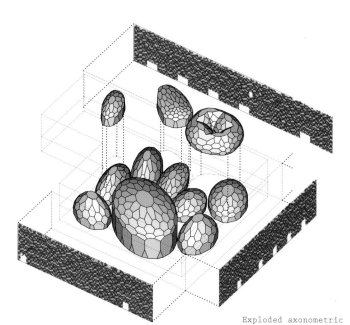

Exploded axonometric

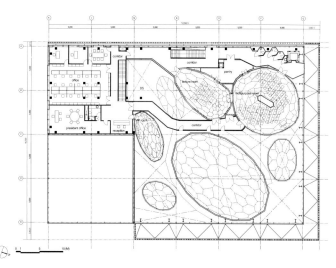

Upper floor plan

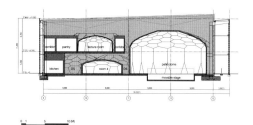

Section A

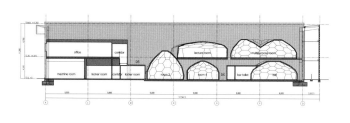

Section B

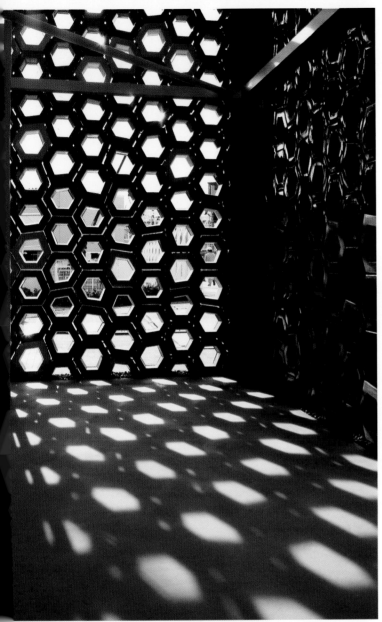

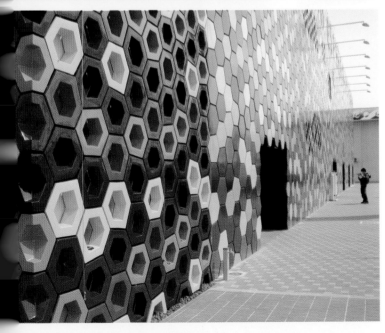

ARCHITECTS: Foreign Office Architects **LOCATION:** Ibaragabasama, Nagakute-cho, Aichi, Japan **DESIGN:** October-December 2003 (competition) February-August 2004 (detail design) **CONSTRUCTION:** September 2004-March 2005 **DESIGN TEAM:** Farshid Moussavi and Alejandro Zaera-Polo with Nerea Calvillo, Izumi Kobayashi, Kensuke Kishikawa, Kenichi Matsuzawa **CLIENT:** Sociedad Estatal para Exposiciones Internacionales (SEEI) **CONTRACTOR:** Takenaka Corporation **PROJECT MANAGER:** Inypsa **STRUCTURAL ENGINEER:** Taro Yokoyama (LOW FAT structure) **SERVICES ENGINEER:** Akeno Engineering Consultants Inc. **FIRE SAFETY ENGINEER:** Akeno Fire Research Institute **CONTENTS DESIGNER:** INGENIA qed **PHOTOGRAPHER:** Satoru Mishima

TILE: 6 distinct hexagonal pieces, plus a regular one for the corner of the building in 6 different colours **DIMENSIONS:** 50 cm in diameter x 12,5 cm high

Award-winner in the 4th Edition of Tile of Spain Awards of Architecture and Interior Design (2005-2006)

Relationships between ceramics and architecture

To clarify why we are involved in the production of ceramics for architecture I would like to make a series of reflections on events that
cannot be ignored, some historical and cultural and others more personal.
Within all the architectural movements that appeared in the western
world at the end of the 19th century and the beginning of the 20th
century, such as Art Nouveau in France, Jugendstil in Germany, Sezession
in Austria, Arts and Graft in England, Art Deco in the USA and the local
variant of Art Nouveau in Catalonia, the relationship between architects
and craftsmen and tradesman is clear as regards the conception and end
result of construction.

     Naturally enough, there existed different approaches within this
interdependence to collaboration between architects and craftsmen.
Some architects wanted to control projects integrally by designing very
precisely all the details of the craftwork in the project. An example
of this way of working is the partnership between Hector Guimard (1867-
1942) and the French ceramicist Alexandre Bigot (1862-1927) when they
built the magnificent stoneware façades of some of the buildings in
Paris. A very different approach to collaboration was adopted by Gaudí
and his associate Jujol, because the latter was allowed a certain amount
of artistic license as can be observed in the fantastic Pedrera building
and the Parc Güell, both in Barcelona.

     It is also worth remembering the fruitful partnerships between
the architect Domènech i Muntaner and the sculptor Pablo Gargallo
during the creation of the sculpted parts of the Hospital de Sant Pau
in Barcelona, and the production of the Pujol i Bausis firm based in
Esplugues de Llobregat just outside Barcelona, destined to produce a
very important portion of the ornamental ceramics used during the Art
Nouveau period in Catalonia.

     With regard to this interaction between architecture and crafts-
manship, I would especially like to mention the Staatliche Bauhaus school
(1919-1933) and its Arts and Crafts teaching centre, which, throughout
its existence, imparted subjects as diverse as ceramics, architecture and
construction, scenography and theatre, under the wing of such renowned
teachers as the architect Walter Gropius, the photographer Moholy-Nagy,
the painters Wassily Kandinsky and Paul Klee, the architects Ludwig Mies
Van de Rohe and Marcel Breuer, etc. One of the objects of the Bauhaus was

to revive the trades and crafts which had a place in construction, place artisanal creativity on a par with the Fine Arts and attempt to commercialise products which, as part of artisanal production, would become consumer goods affordable for the general public.

On a much more personal level and thanks to the connections which my father, the artist Antoni Cumella, had in the world of art in general and the world of architecture in particular, I was able to closely experience this interrelationship between the crafts and architecture. He was co-founder of the Group R together with the architects and designers Moragas, Sostres, Bohigas, Martorell, Gili, Pratmarsó and others, and they organised the exhibition "Industry and Architecture" (1954), which encouraged contact between construction companies and the artists who defended the so-called "integration of the arts". According to Daniel Giralt Miracle, this event was the embryo of ADIFAD (1960), which was the first association of industrial designers in Spain.

Later, between 1959 and 1962 at the seat of FAD, Alexandre Cirici, Romà Vallès and Antoni Cumella set up an art school inspired in the principles of the Bauhaus which fomented knowledge of tools and materials, the study of space and colours, the importance of composition and systems of construction, and the integration of the arts into architecture.

On the death of my father in 1985, I decided that the familiar business should actively focus on the production of ceramics for architectural applications, without excluding other options. Two architects had a decisive influence on me from the start: One was Josep Maria Botey who, thanks to his advice and criticism and his suggestion that I be allowed to make a small contribution to the restoration of Gaudi's Casa Batlló, paved the way to work in the restoration of Catalan Art Nouveau works as important as the Parc Güell by Gaudí and the Hospital de Sant Pau by Domènech i Muntaner. The other architect was Cristian Cirici. Through working with him, I was able to meet the architects Oscar Tusquets, Lluís Clotet, Pep Bonet and Enric Steegman, who together with Cirici formed the estudi PER, and this gave me the opportunity to establish contacts with many other architects.

The production of Ceràmica Cumella has been determined by the desire to work with stoneware fired at high temperatures (1,250º C) — provided that the pieces are fixed on the exterior of buildings, and

1 Guaranty Building, Buffalo, (1894-1896) by Louis Sullivan. Photographer: Crombie Taylor

2 Mural by Antoni Cumella at the head offices of Novartis, Barcelona (1972) by Burckhardt-Busquets.

also by the desire not to lose the opportunity to exploit their third dimension, i.e., volume. For this reason we work with different methods of production, so that we can choose the most suitable manufacturing process depending on the pieces we have to produce. The pastes and glazes, which we always make ourselves, mark the final appearance of many of the projects in which we have collaborated. We consider that the future of the trade lies in an open attitude to new technologies without losing sight of past reference points. Naturally, the pieces must be manufactured in compliance with the current standards.

This constant contact with the world of architecture led to work with Enric Miralles and Benedetta Tagliabue when they were designing the Parc dels Colors de Mollet, the Parc de Diagonal Mar and the Santa Caterina market. I have fond memories of the joint work done on these projects — their inception and the many long hours spent at their studio. It was very enjoyable to observe their way of working. The design of the roof of the Santa Caterina Market was particularly interesting. The idea was to echo the colours of the fruits and vegetables in the market by creating a sort of large-dimension pixelated image (5.500 m2). At the outset, it was decided that the pieces should be hexagonal, because this was the shape best adapted to the curvature of the different parts of the roof. Simultaneously, we worked on the image. The difficulty here resided in the fact that the pattern was designed digitally on a computer screen. Finally, we selected 67 colours. These colours were then printed out on paper and used as a blueprint for the development in the laboratory of ceramic glazes whose range of colours was as close to the originals as possible. Because of the different transformations that colours undergo in function of the surface they are applied to, analysis of colour samples is always carried out subjectively: a computer screen where the image is displayed as a slide, high quality printing on paper to obtain a solid image, and the end result is a ceramic glaze fired at high temperature (1.250ºC). During the whole process it was vital to try to visualise the end result globally, so as to respect the intensity and tonal differences of the various colour palettes.

To facilitate the fixing of the ceramic pieces we designed a series of modules made up of 37 hexagons, 15 cm thick and all the same colour, fixed to a backing of vinyl mesh using a polyurethane hot melt adhesive. These modules were delivered to the site numbered and ordered according to the corresponding pattern which would be created on each of the seven sections of the roof. It should be mentioned that the structure and the supporting surface which received the ceramic modules is wholly made of waterproof timber with two layers of polyurethane, an important detail as regards the innovative use of the ceramics.

One of our most recent projects was the Spanish Pavilion at the Aichí Expo, Japan, designed by Foreign Office Architects. Owing to the large number of pieces that had to be manufactured and the demanding deadline, we carried out this project in conjunction with the firm Ceràmica Decorativa: the modeller Claudi de José was responsible for the models and the moulding. As it was impossible to comment the details of the project face-to-face on a regular basis, because the architects' studio is in London, we had to communicate via Internet: The glazes were developed using the Pantone samples sent by email and the resulting tile samples were delivered by post. The AutoCAD plans tra-velled from London to Spain via Japan because it fell to the Japanese construction company to send them to us.

The façade is like a skin which surrounds the building, in which there are some opaque parts formed by flat hexagonal pieces and other perforated areas where the pieces — similarly hexagonal — form a lattice visible from both sides. These latticework pieces are attached by means of staples fixed too a metal structure concealed between two pieces, one on the inside and one on the outside of the building. It should be mentioned that this structure, like a honeycomb but formed by irregular hexagons, is built using six different pieces in six colours. Through the repetition of a set of six pieces but interchanging the colours, there is no perceptible repeated pattern in the eye of the observer. The only geometrically regular pieces are the ones used to form the corners of the building, from where the façades made up of irregular pieces lead off.

Lastly, I would like to remark that this way of understanding ceramics, i.e., its implications in architecture and the possibility of using different systems of production, has renewed architects' confidence in the use of ceramics in their projects. Reciprocally, their demand for ceramic products has reaffirmed our belief in the notion of ceramics applied to architecture.

TONI CUMELLA I VENDRELL His interest in ceramics is linked to the family ceramics workshop owned by his father, the ceramicist Antoni Cumella. He studied industrial engineering at the University of Barcelona (1968) and photography at the Institut d'Estudis Fotogràfics de Catalunya (1970).
He has been dedicated to ceramics production since 1970. In 1985, he began to steer the family business towards the production of ceramics applied to architecture. He participated in the restoration of the Casa Batlló and the Parc Güell by Gaudí, and also the Ricarda house by Antoni Bonet. In addition, he produced the ceramics for projects such as the restoration of the Santa Caterina Market by EMTB and the Spanish Pavilion at the Aichí Expo (Japan) by Foreign Office Architects.
He collaborated with the Chair of Ceramic Studies at the International University of Catalonia during 2004-2005.

Ceramics: material for a sustainable paradise

A mythological reference common to almost all cultures and particularly to the written religions is the memory of the lost paradise: a place where humanity experienced its maximum physical and spiritual plenitude.

Never mind that humanity was reduced to just two individuals, who were not even able to write and pass down their story. In reality, if this story has reached us, something similar to a paradise must have existed to create an oral tradition, which was later recorded by scribes, the precursors of modern chroniclers. They used clay tablets baked in the sun, the first ceramic pieces. The fact that paradise has always been described as being between two rivers, and the knowledge that one of the first cultures to leave written evidence of its first myths was in ancient Mesopotamia, has lead many experts to the conclusion that this earthly paradise was situated between the Tigris and the Euphrates in the area of the devastated modern-day country of Iraq. However, a journey to the region, at the height of summer with an average temperature of 37ºC and maximums of 50ºC in the shade, is enough to refute this belief, and there is no historical evidence of a climatic change which might suggest that this crude reality is a recent occurrence. So Paradise will have to be situated somewhere else, perhaps not so far away.

Zoroaster, founder of the oldest known written religion, Zoroastrianism, with its one god Ahura Mazda, was the first to mention the lost paradise. His religion, described in a book of which there are only remain fragments, collects together multiple beliefs, stories and myths from his surroundings. Zoroastro lived in the region of modern-day Iran, so the search for Paradise should begin in Persia.

The North of Persia is confined between rivers, near the Caspian Sea and the Elburz mountain range, and isolated by these and Kurdistan from the rest of the country. It is a fertile land with a gentle tropical climate, and turns out to be, not just the most likely, but the only place which matches the vision of paradise. Considering that it has been invaded systematically by successive waves of nomadic tribes from central and northern Asia, it is quite probable that the sword of Damocles, the exterminating angel, came in the guise of one of the predecessors of Kublai Khan, who must have forced the inhabitants to flee over the mountains and settle in the barren Farsi plateaux. The primitive inhabitants, driven out of their native land, not only did not forget the lost paradise, but also tried as hard as they could to recreate it.

So, to solve the serious shortage of water, they built extensive networks of qanats (canals laid out underground to prevent evaporation, which carried water from the mountains for hundreds of kilometres). Thanks to these they were able to convert stretches of simple desert into authentic artificial oases. For the construction and upkeep of the qanats it was essential, in order to maintain the constant flow of water along a gentle slope, to dig deep wells for their regulation and construct tunnel vaults in areas of unstable terrain. As there were no alternatives at the time, the material used for these wells and vaults was ceramic brick or twice-baked adobe, ceramic materials which have lasted down to the present day.

On the other hand, these brick vaults were not a new system of construction: they were derived from the so-called false vaults which had existed since ancient times and gradually perfected until they became an inherent part of the architectural landscape. They contain a wealth of different bonds and other structural solutions that still fascinate visitors today.

In this search for sustainability in the new Persian environment, once secured the water supply — and this was the first touch of paradise — it remained to find a method to mitigate the effects of the high summer temperatures in the interior of the huts where they lived, made of adobe or rammed earth (earth dried for better or worse by a relentless sun). So they devised a system of ventilation. They invented wind

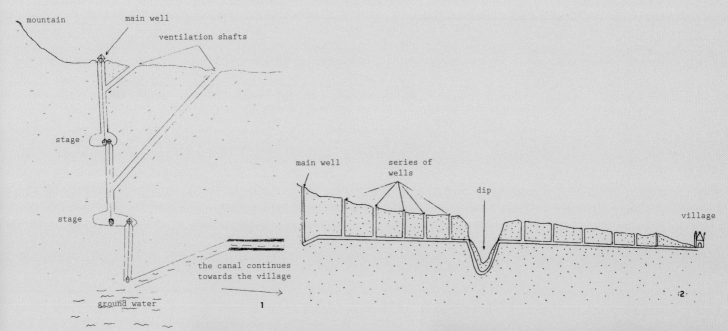

1 Sketch of main well

2 Sketch of the Qanats

3 Well entrance

4 Yazd, ice house entrance

5 Ventilation tower

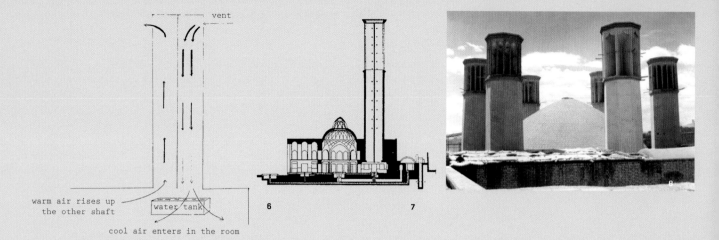

vent

warm air rises up
the other shaft

water tank

cool air enters in the room

6   7

6   Sketch ventilation tower

7   Section of ventilation tower

8   Yazd, cistern with 6 'bagdirs'
      (ventilation towers)

towers: slender towers built with dried earth, anything from rammed earth blocks to the most sophisticated ceramics, and perforated vertically by a number of air flues designed to cool down the insides of the buildings. According to Somar Odnan these towers normally have a square base with sides measuring from 1,5 to 2,5 m, and a height-to-side ratio ranging from 6 to 9, so they generally vary in height from 9 y 15 m.

These structures can be subdivided into four sections:
* Load-bearing basement, corresponding in size to the interiors to be cooled down, seperate from the tower but benefiting from its air-conditioning effects.
* Main structure, generally quadrilateral, with solid, blank, outside walls, subdivided on the inside into between four to eight flues with a triangular cross-section, by means of vertical partitions laid out crosswise, or radially on an octagonal plane.
* A crown of vertical ceramic slats supported by the main structure, whose four to eight flues (here ventilated laterally) extend into this section.
* Roof, normally a square flat slab, slight overhanging the slats.

From sunrise to sunset at least one side of the tower is always bathed in sunlight. The ceramic slats on the sunny side, which increase the surface area exposed to the sun, function like a radiator, which then warms up the upper levels of air in the adjacent flue. This air tends to rise, so producing an ascending air stream. Because of the relative difference in pressure in the basement, cooler air is then sucked through from the flues on the shady sides. The Venturi effect generates a constant flow of air which passes through the inside of the building, thus helping to make it cooler and more comfortable. In quite a few cases, there is also a flue which communicates with an underground qanat, so that the air is further cooled down by contact with the cold underground water, thus making the system more efficient.
The large number of these beautiful, sophisticated, self-sustaining and, paradoxically, primitive installations has given the desert cities an airy skyline: slender towers with long vertical ceramic slats breaking up the horizon.
     The search for sustainability by those descendants of paradise did not terminate here. The basic writing surface, the sun-baked clay tablet, was made from the most abundant material available with no

expense of energy during its manufacture. Once finshed with, the tablets were returned to the earth they came from, recycled without producing any environmental impact.

On the other hand, tablets which were of special interest and worth preserving were baked in wood-fired kilns, thus converting them into real durable ceramic pieces.

The profoundest thoughts, greatest events, most significant stanzas and finest verses of that ancient culture were immortalised on those beautiful ceramic tablets. The illustrations accompanying this article give just a small idea of their skilful workmanship and delicate colouring.

And, speaking of beauty, the transformation of the walls and magnificent cupolas of the mosques, by adorning them with interlaced letters in serene and indecipherable patterns which cite the thousand names of the lord of all paradises, makes ceramics the sublimest of all messengers, the most transcendent of doorways: for a practising Moslem the door of a mosque is, so to speak, the door to paradise.

Is this the reason why the muqarabia at the doors of the mosques and madrasahs are reminiscent of the stalagmites at the entrance to a cave? Might not this cave be an unconscious and nostalgic abstraction of the cave which was home, once upon a time, to the first human beings in that paradise? We cannot be sure, but what we do know is that the material which their descendents used to recreate a sustainable paradise was ceramics in all its many forms.

9 General view of Yazd

10-15 Isfahan

FERNANDO JUAN RAMOS GALINO is Doctor of Architecture and Professor of the Departamento de Construcción Arquitectónica of the Escuela Técnica Superior de Arquitectura de Barcelona, of which he was Director from 1984 to 1991. His most important projects include the reconstruction of Mies Van der Rohe's Pavilion in Barcelona and the Museum of Modern Art in Barcelona in partnership with Richard Meier. He is currently General Speaker for the UNESCO-UIA Council for Education in Architecture.

ANNA RAMOS SANZ is a practising architect and tutor of architecture in Barcelona. She collaborated in the design of the corporative headquarters of Boehringer Ingelheim in Sant Cugat (Barcelona) and the restoration of the Casino in Rubí (Barcelona). She is currently President of the Asociación de Jóvenes Arquitectos de Catalunya (Assocation of Young Architects of Catalonia).

Café Una
Vienna, Austria

The context stretches from Messepalast to the Museumsquartier. The location is the site of the former imperial stables. The architecture is military-like, severe, hard, authoritarian. Even the sky is framed and disciplined in the courtyards.

The previous appropriation of the area by the artists was reactionary, opportunistic, impertinent, invasive, rebellious, easy going, constantly modified, and always changing.

Then came the project of the Museumsquartier. It was a heavyweight, 15 years of decisions, studies, and construction site.

Why is it that usually things become rigid and freeze as soon as architecture manifests itself? One does not live any more, one looks, one moves from the side of the players to that of the spectators, to the "museification", from refutation to official art, from the ephemeral to the definitive.

The cafeteria project of the cafeteria in the Architekturzentrum Wien is like an act of resistance against the official project of the Museumsquartier. It is supposed to be different through its lightness and liveliness — just as it was before. It seemed as if only a big blue sky was needed, a kind of shift into another world, into a dream.

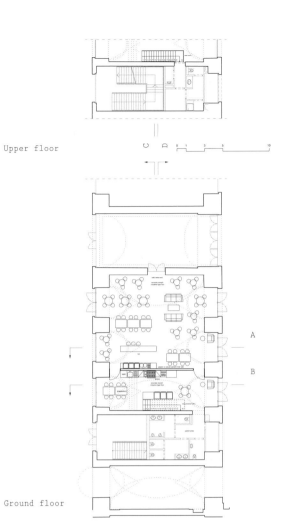

Upper floor

Ground floor

A

B

Cross section A

Cross section B

Long section C

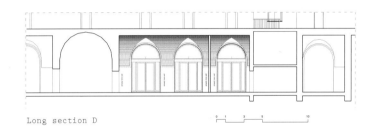

Long section D

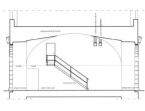

ARCHITECTS: Lacaton & Vassal architectes **LOCATION:** Architektur Zentrum, Vienna, Austria **IMPLEMENTATION:** 2001 **DESIGN TEAM:** Anne Lacaton and Jean Philippe Vassal with Mathieu Laporte, David Pradel **SITE ARCHITECT:** Stephan Seehof, Vienna **CLIENT:** Architecktur Zentrum Wien **PHOTOGRAPHER:** Rupert Steiner

TILE DESIGN: Asiye Kolbai-Kafalier, artist, Vienna

Pleasure Garden of the Utilities
Stoke on Trent, England

Bespoke street furniture made in collaboration with the fireclay team from the local Armitage Shanks factory in the town. We chose to use ceramics in part because Stoke on Trent is the centre of the ceramics industry in Britain but also due to an interest in using a material that is associated with fragility. The scheme brings to the public street a scale of domestic intimacy and delicacy in a situation where there is unfounded anxiety about the town centre as meeting place and the potential for public disorder. Some of the young men who gather here also work in the factory where these 4 metre long benches are made.

They are complemented by silver birch trees and lighting.

The tile was a one-off bespoke item produced in the factory with artist's members of muf architecture/art.

ARCHITECTS: muf LOCATION: City centre Hanley, Stoke
on Trent, England COMPLETION: June 1999 DESIGN TEAM:
Liza Fior, Katherine Clarke, Cathy Hawley, Ashley
McCormick CLIENT: Stoke City Council

TILE DESIGN: muf architecture

Study for new applications of ceramics in construction

Since 1993, CRAFT, the "Research Centre for the Arts of Fire and Earth", has been organising workshops with artists, architects and designers for research into new application possibilities for ceramic materials, especially in construction.

Fascinated by the wide range of applications of this material, comprehensive research began including elements from a great variety of design fields: tableware decorative elements, structural aspects of tile and mosaic production, application of the particular chemical properties of ceramics (high fire resistance, protection against abrasion, light reflection, etc.), and historical connotations in the use of ceramics.

After much questioning at the beginning of the project study, the concept developed into coating steel support columns in order to increase their fire resistant properties. In this study, numerous technical and aesthetic aspects came together: the performance of ceramics in fire, the thermal properties of reflecting materials, absorption and reverberation, aesthetic and decorative properties like lustre, motifs and fragility. This idea emerged from the design issues faced at the time of the Palais de Tokyo project in Paris.

The prototype of a steel column coated with ceramics has been produced. Various tests for fire resistance have been carried out and prove the system to be feasible. Once the problems of fixing ceramic to steel and ceramic to ceramic are resolved, this new type of material combination will go into mass production.

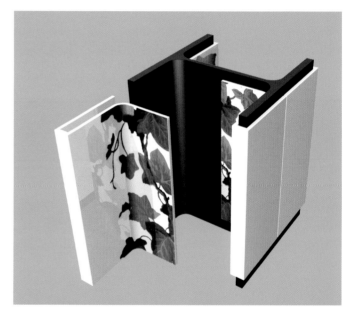

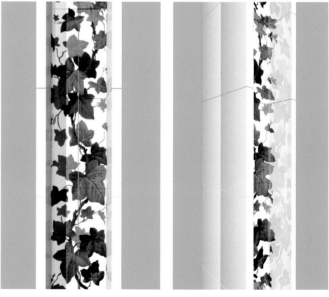

Section of a HEA 180 steel beam

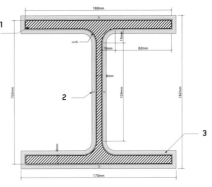

1 HEA 180 steel HP-profile

2 Joint

3 Ceramic element protecting the HP-profile

Section of the assembling process of the ceramic
element on the HEA 180 steel column

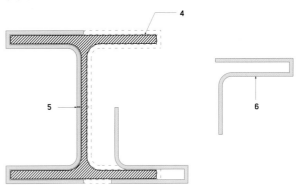

4 The unprotected profile is 15' fireproof, which is not
   sufficient for most structures.

5 Joint

6 Ceramic element approximately 5 mm thick glued to
   the column. It works as a fireproof element akin to an
   intumescent paint or to plaster.
   Tests should be carried out to determine its integrity
   at 30', 60', 90'.

ARCHITECTS: Lacaton & Vassal architectes WORKSHOP: 2002
DESIGN TEAM: Anne Lacaton and Jean Philippe Vassal with
David Pradel CLIENT: CRAFT (Research Centre for the
Arts of Fire and Earth), Limoges, France PHOTO: CRAFT

Bush Houses

Land-Arch Indeed, we have long been interested in this possibility of manipulating construction and nature to obtain new hybrid 'anti-types': topographies, reliefs, geographies or new 'vegetations'.

The project of *Ceramic Network* allows us to develop an overall concept where varius apporximations will combine, linked around the ideas of habitat, construction and landscape. The idea is to include in the design not only inhabitable space, but also transitional layers between inside and outside.

The old topos of 'old-purpose-ivy' or 'camouflage' would give way to a genuine 'climbing-plant' house, inert and alive, solid and light. A mixed marriage of ceramic lattice and organic tissue.

A house like a huge bush or a little aglomeration.

Bush Houses In this sense, the Bush-Houses extrapolate from the possibility of imagining an inhabited environment as a large organic cnstruction or a mineral landscape.

Latice in a Lattice The design of this project led us to forsee a 120 x 60 cm ceramic piece used as façade element. The 120 x 60 cm size allows one to work with two modules of a standard height of 2,4 metres. For reasons of fabrication, the realisation of the piece was reduced to a 60 x 60 cm format, a module that can be applied both horizontally and vertically.

The piece is a 'composite' uniting the arranged metallic structure and the ceramic support lattice. This allows one to create strong façade elements that attach nature to the edifice and equip it with thermal insulation.

The consecutive phases of trial and error concerning the number and distribution of empty space, the mass and the range of colors (greens), the size of the piece and its lateral adjustments, as well as various other experiments, were the principle challenges of a project both elementary and complex.

ALICER's work was essential, as well as technical support from the ceramic tiles manufacturers.

The idea of the bush as a volumetric element obtained not only from the landscaped model but also from architectonic construction can now take on all its value.

Land-Arch returns!

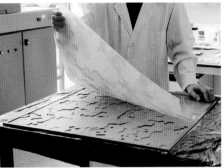

ARCHITECTS: ACTAR Arquitectura **WORKSHOP:** 2002
DESIGN TEAM: Manuel Gausa and Florence Raveau with
Vicky Lenz, Kazuyo Nishida, Bebo Ferlito, Luisa
Riveiro, Nicolas Petillon, Mathilde Félix-Faure,
Judith Gessler, François Martín, Marta Frazão,
Moritz Linde-Boldt, Roland Stutz **CLIENT:** CRAFT
(Research Centre for the Arts of Fire and Earth),
Limoges, France **PHOTOGRAPHER:** Jean-Christophe Dupuy

Ceramic prototypes: new applications

The following series of prototypes are the result of R + D by Alicer.

CERAMIC SHELVING

Ceramic shelving is a wall tile system (1) that incorporates a glass, timber or plastic shelf, thus performing two functions cladding for walls and support for objects.
The shelf is fitted into a specially designed tile.
The novelty of this tile collection ceramic lies in the incorporation of a shelf.

1 Key pieces that comprise the system and the sequence of anchoring the shelf to the tiles.

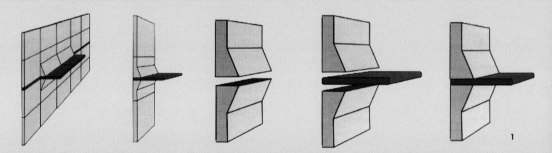

1

The basic support piece is a wedge-shaped tile.
Two of these pieces are mortared to the wall, with the flat edges of the wedges facing each other.
The shelf is then fitted snugly between the pieces, forcing them apart. The space between the pieces is filled in with a decorative strip of the same material as the shelf.

INDOOR DRY TILING SYSTEM

This tiling system is applicable to all types of walls (2). The tiles are hung from a substructure of two vertical guides.
The tile is fixed directly to the wall by means of a metal brace plate, fixed to the wall by the upper part and adhered by the lower part to the back of the tile. At the same time the tile is supported and plumbed on two vertical metal guides, which, together with a smaller metal positioning plate, adhered to the base of the tile, ensures the correct positioning of the tile on the wall.

The tiles are fitted from the bottom of the wall upwards, with each successive tile covering the top of the metal brace plate of the tile below.

This system requires less labour than the traditional method of tiling, eliminating the need for a coat of cement mortar on the wall, skilled labour for laying the tiles and the use of adhesives, as well as generating a considerably smaller volume of waste material. With this new system tiling is a clean job that can be done by an unskilled person.

Another feature of the system to bear in mind is the ease and speed with which the fitted tiles can be removed and refitted, without any additional work. To create new compositions, the user only has to remove the metal brace plates and remount them wherever required.

The tiling system (1) consists of three metal components which ensure a firm, tight ceramic tile skin: two vertical metal guides (8) per tile, an upper anchoring (2) which fixes the tile to the wall, and a lower anchoring (5) for correct positioning of the tile on the surface.

The rectangular hollow section vertical guides (8) come with two rubber strips (7) running lengthwise along the guides, on which the tiles rest, and which seal the wall and ensure the stability of the tiles.

The metal brace plate (2) is bent back and out at top (3) to create a flange, which has two holes for fixing the plate to the wall with fasteners. The design of this plate is such that once it is fixed to both the tile and the wall, the plate is in tension, pressing the tile lightly against vertical guides. The posts are fixed to the wall and plumbed with a suitable number of fasteners.

The positioning plate (5) is rectangular in shape and has a rubber strip (6) on the lower part. This plate is adhered to the base of the tile and ensures the anchoring of the upper piece to the lower piece.

PERMEABLE EXTERIOR PAVING TILE

This system uses a rectangular or square section paving tile with an irregular pattern of holes running all the way through it and which allow water to drain through quickly to the lower layers of the paving system. At the same time, since water does not collect on the surface, it offers better purchase in wet conditions.

Two variations on the system are described. In the first type of execution (**3**) the paving tile is the result of a cluster of cylinders (1) of varying diameters, arranged in parallel to each other and to the thickness of the tile. The form of the paving tile is a block of flat, square section faces in which the thickness (2) is less at the edges (3).

The arrangement of the cylinders in the block is such that several blocks can be joined at their edges and fit snugly together with broken or straight joints.

In the second type of execution, (**4**) the paving tile is made up of a cluster of spheres (4) of varying diameters, also in a block of flat, square section faces in which the thickness (5) is less at the edges (6). The edges of the paving tile are designed such that they fit together with broken or straight joints to compose a paved surface.

2 Indoor dry tiling system complete with the tile.

3 and 4 Examples of two ways of executing the paving tile resulting from a cluster of cylinders of varying diameters and another resulting from a cluster of spheres.

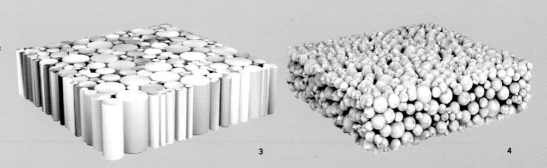

3   4

INTEGRATED BACK-LIT SIGNAGE SYSTEM FOR WALL AND FLOOR TILES

This system provides a back-lit solution for signage in walls and floors (**5a and 5b**). In consists of a fibre optic tube with lateral light emission, fed by a light source, that back-lights tiles out of which the desired forms have been cut to let the light through.

The fibre optic tube is located between the tiles and the surface they cover, protected throughout its length by a duct or a U-shaped profile. The desired signage is cut out of the tiles and the opening is sealed with a solid, durable transparent or translucent material, either glass or resin-based.

The integrated back-lit signage system for walls and floors, in one of its forms, consists of three elements to ensure correct functioning: cut-out tile (1), duct (2), and fibre optic tube (3).

Cut-out tile (1). The desired signage (circles, arrows, etc.) is drawn on the tile before cutting, and that part is laid over the fibre optic tube (4) previously fitted in the wall.

The openings are filled with transparent or translucent material to seal the tile while allowing the light from the fibre optic tube to shine through.

The duct (2) must be long enough to house the fibre optic tube over the length of the signage, U-shaped and fixed to and flush with the wall (4). The open side of the duct faces outwards so that the tube can be housed in it without blocking the light cast through the cut-out tile.

The dimensions of the duct (2) will vary: in length, according to the span; and in width, according to the area of the tile (1) to be back-lit.

Fibre optic tube (3) composed of several specially treated optic fibres to give maximum lateral light emission and protected by a transparent housing.

This sort of tube carries light from a light source along its length emitting lateral light, which in this case is cast through holes cut out of the tiles (1).

The fibre optic tube (3) gets its light from a source at one of its ends. To get a brighter light all along the tube (3) both ends can be connected to a light source.

5a Components of the back-lit signage system for walls and floor.

5b Model for testing the system.

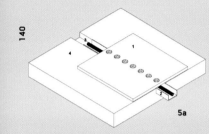

5a

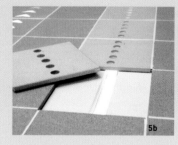

5b

CERAMIC WALL TILES WITH CONCEALED JOINTS

This ceramic wall tiling with concealed joints uses two types of overlapping tiles: a rectangular piece and a circular or elliptical piece. The rectangular pieces are laid in a staggered pattern to form a base with spaces into which fit the circular or elliptical pieces.

On the back of the non-rectangular piece there is a projection of the same dimensions as the rectangular pieces, which fits into the spaces between the latter. The non-rectangular pieces then cover the joints in the base.

Once all the tiles have been laid, they comprise a pattern of rounded forms touching each other at four points over a tile base without visible joints between the pieces.

Below we describe the configurations of the ceramic wall tiling with concealed joints seen in the illustrations. These are only two of several possible configurations.

In the first configuration (**6 and 7**) the tiles that form the base are square and flat (1). The rounded pieces (2) that cover the base pieces are circular, with a diameter equal to the diagonal of the square base pieces, with rounded edges and with a square projection on back (3) of

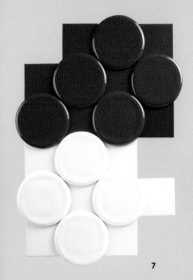

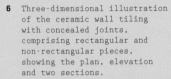

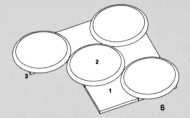

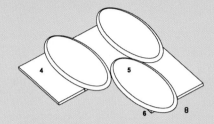

7

6 Three-dimensional illustration of the ceramic wall tiling with concealed joints, comprising rectangular and non-rectangular pieces, showing the plan, elevation and two sections.

7 Ceramic wall tiling with concealed joints comprising rectangular and circular pieces.

8 Three-dimensional illustration of the ceramic wall tiling with concealed joints comprising rectangular and elliptical pieces.

equal dimensions to the base piece, inscribed in the circle and significantly smaller and thinner than the main part of the tile. In the second configuration (**8**) the tiles that form the base are rectangular and flat (4). The curved pieces (5) that cover the base pieces describe an ellipse with rounded edges and a rectangular projection on the back (6) of equal dimensions to the base piece, inscribed in the ellipse and smaller and thinner than the main part of the tile.

COVERED-JOINT TILING FOR CURVED SURFACES

The tiling consists of a single piece specially designed (not only) for covering surfaces with a single curvature.

The adaptability to a curved surface is determined by the curved forms that define the tile at two opposite edges. Each of the longitudinal edges of the tile has a different form, such that, if we overlap two pieces along their longitudinal edges, they can rotate on each other without losing the overlap. Thus they can cover the curved surface without revealing the joint perpendicular to the radius of the curvature.

The arrangement of the tiles can be either vertical or horizontal, depending only on the direction of the curve to cover, and they can be fitted on a mesh or with traditional bonding.

Below we describe the configuration of the ceramic wall tiling with concealed joints (**9 and 10**). This is only one of several possible configurations for the tile (1), which is for cladding curved walls with covered joints. The tile is defined by its transversal section, since it is produced by the extrusion of that section.

The body that forms the transversal section contains three parts: a central part (3), consisting of an elongated rectangle, the width of which is very narrow relative to its length, and two unequal parts (2 and 4) at either end of the central part (3).

The left part is capped with a circular sector (4), half of which is fused with the central part (3) while the other half forms an overhang. The right end (2) is formed by somewhat more than a quarter circle, which is fused by one of its straight edges to the right end of the

9 Piece that forms the covered-joint tiling for curved surfaces.

10 Prototype

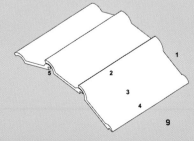

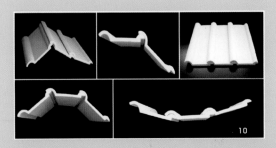

rectangular part (3). The interior circumference of the right end (2) has a radius slightly greater than that of the circular sector of the left end (4); this design enables the two ends to slide over each other when two tiles are overlapped, with the lower left vertex (5) of the central rectangle acting as the centre of rotation for both pieces.

TILING WITH HIDDEN AND SEALED JOINTS FOR SLOPED SURFACES

The tiling with hidden and sealed joints for sloped surfaces comprises a single model of square tile with a projection at one of its corners that is laid in a stepped pattern without leaving open joints or openings between the pieces in the direction of the slope from which rainwater might enter (**11**).

The design succeeds in combining the aesthetic effect of a decorated flat surface and the functionality required for cladding on a sloped surface(**12**).

The cladding consists of one model of very thin, square tile (1). The tile has two contiguous sharp edges (3) and two contiguous rounded edges (2). The corners where a rounded edge meets a sharp edge are chamfered (4), while the corners where two equal edges meet form a right angle.

In the corner formed by the two rounded edges (2) the tile features a projection from its underside (5) of length equal to the thickness of the tile and whose section is that of a triangle with curved hypotenuse: It has two concave faces, which fit snugly around the rounded edges of the tile below, and one convex face that describes a radial surface equal to the thickness of the piece.

CURVED PERIMETER TILING SYSTEM

Hydraulic-cut porcelain stoneware floor tiles.

The paving comprises three pieces of different sizes that fit together to form a continuous surface (**13 and 14**). The largest piece is a figure-8 with loops of equal size joined by curved segments: its design using solely curved lines lends it a sinuous appearance.

The other two pieces are used to fill in the spaces left between the main pieces when fitted together. One is a disc that fits into the circular holes in each main piece, and the other is a rhombus with convex sides that fits into the spaces between every four main pieces.

11 Tiling with hidden and sealed joints for sloped surfaces.

12 Prototype

13 Assembled tiles

14 Detail of the system

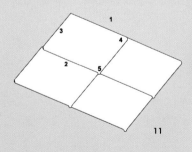

CALIDOSCOPIO

Calidoscopio (**15 and 16**) is a tile mosaic system that consists of a multiple matching pattern module comprised of seven different, irregular pieces. It is designed for covering large surfaces, although it can also be laid in strips. It is conceived of as a means of achieving a visual result similar to that of trencadís — cladding fashioned out of shards of odd coloured tiles.

The choice of a hexagon as the shape has the following advantages:
- It provides flush, close-fitting flooring.
- It can be rotated more than any other shape, thus providing greater visual variation.

The module obtained with the assembly of the seven different pieces can be placed in six different positions, meaning that the number of possible combinations is extremely high (n6, with n being the number of combined modules). Moreover, the arrangement of the coloured pieces offers another level of the possibilities, adding even greater personal touch to the end-product.
This project was awarded an Honourable Mention at the 4th International Ceramics Competition '95 in Mino, Japan.

15 Calidoscopio

16 Detail of the system

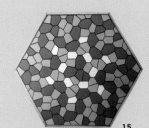

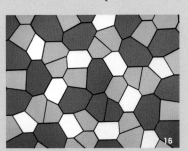

15

16

MILA PAYÁ has a degree in Ceramics from the Valencia School of Art. She specialized in ceramic cladding at the Gaetano Ballardini Institute in Faenza (Italy). She has been a member of ALICER since its founding in 1993. For the past ten years she has directed the ALICER tendencies department and since 1988 has taught Industrial Decorative Technologies at the Escola d'Art i Superior de Disseny de Castelló.

Architecture proposes ceramics

Lately, architects have been receiving a good deal of information from ceramics manufacturers about the possibilities offered by ceramic tiles in ventilated façades, pavements, interior finishes — products developed for today's architecture. But architects must also provide the manufacturers with new ideas — for new dimensions, applications and uses.

This is exactly what the Chair of Ceramic Studies proposes to do. Sponsored by ASCER (Spanish Ceramic Tile Manufacturers' Association), and launched in October 2004 at the School of Architecture of the International University of Catalonia, it brings together architects and ceramic tile makers. Its main focus is on teaching, although it also works with the private sector in publishing, consulting and R+D programmes. In the teaching realm, architecture students engage in a broad range of activities: technological expositions in which the manufacturers supplement the future architects' training with technical knowledge of their products and their possibilities; conferences by architects who stand out for their imaginative application of ceramic material in their works; visits to manufacturing facilities; and, of course, projects in which the students develop dimensions and applications or experiment with existing tile dimensions in new spaces. The work by these students is then assessed by a special jury made up of prestigious architects.

The projects, done during the 2004-2005 academic year, were presented in four groups: cells, folds, hybrids and pivoting.

<u>Cells</u> are flat paving tiles, in this case arranged in patterns different from the traditional bidirectional reticule; variable units of several pieces, like the cells of an organism, where the interest lies in how they relate to each other. They are used in pavements, as in the works by Carles Flotats (1) and Joan Sistach (2).

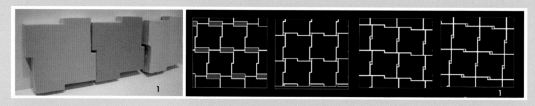

Folds are tiles whose planeity is altered. With new folding technologies, one can manipulate the topology, creating an unexpected dimensional complexity in the pieces. This can generate a range of furnishings or finishes, as seen in the works by Javier Pequeño (**3**), Jesús Asensio (**4**), Mirem Etxezarreta (**5**) or Daniel Poch (**6**).

Pivoting are pieces that show a large faceted volumetry around a pivotal axis. They are found in pergolas or lattice and in general on façades whose surface varies with respect to the vanishing point of the observer, as seen in the works by Marc Medina (**7**) and Laura Carballés (**8**).

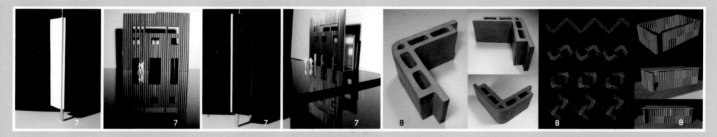

Hybrids are pieces that are added to, juxtaposed or combined with other materials to create new technological possibilities. With air or expanded polystyrene bubbles one can make panels with cavities and rough textures fit for lattice or noise-absorbing applications, as in the works by Jonathan Arnabat (**9**) and Natalia Manzanas (**10**). On the other hand, Jaume Colom, for example, used polyvinyl butyral film to make layered ceramic pieces similar to plywood or laminated safety glass (**11**).

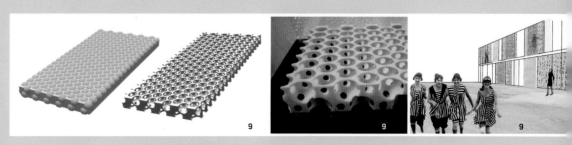

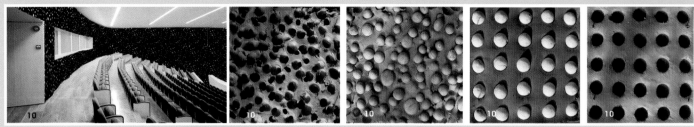

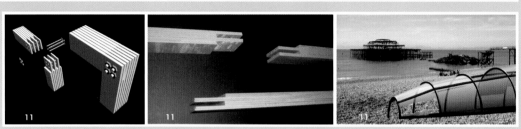

These efforts are not isolated from the industrial reality. New products are conceived that interest manufacturers. This I saw for myself at the 3rd Casa Barcelona, during the 2005 Construmat construction fair, where I was invited to design two systems made with large pieces of porcelain stoneware: versatile slats made by Saloni Cerámica and the Brico-aplacados (DIY cladding) made by Roca Cerámica.

The versatile slats (**12**): In our Mediterranean climate there has always been a great architectural interest in solar control systems using lattices and slats — for the quality of the filtered light, for their vibrant presence in the composition of façades, and for their considerable cooling effect. Here a material like porcelain stoneware offers significant advantages in terms of weathering resistance: it is maintenance-free and dimensionally and chromatically stable against moisture and sun.

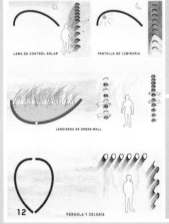

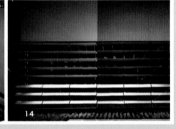

With Saloni we presented a solar control system on façade and roof enclosures based on applications of porcelain stoneware slats. The novelty of the idea lies in that, with the new technologies for folding paving tiles, you can create a specific curved profile (**13**). The piece is applicable to a range of uses, while it also lends material continuity with the opaque pieces of the enclosure clad with the flat pieces of the same material (**14**). In addition, the bending makes the slat much more resistant to flexing and reduces the need for steel reinforcement.

The main application is as a solar filter, both on glazed areas of areas façades and in intermediate spaces between the exterior and the interior of the house (courtyards, porches, balconies). The same slat that during the day provides shade from the sun (**15**) at night can

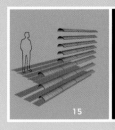

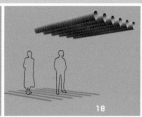

provide light: its curved profile acts as a shade for bulbs fitted in the concave part (**16**).

The versatility of such slats extends to other uses, such as plant pots: several fitted on a vertical can make a *"green wall"* (**17**), an interesting botanical façade with plants, such as aromatics or sedums, that require little watering. The rigidity that the bending lends to the piece also makes it applicable for pergolas or fencing (**18**), taking us far beyond its original use on façades.

<u>DIY dry-fitted tiles</u> (**19**): Do It Yourself might be seen as an alternative to traditional construction. In such conditions, porcelain stoneware is a sort of wild-card material with manifold uses and in manifold situations, and one which offers a great variety of appearances. But, in dealing with non-professional builders, a simple and adaptable fitting system becomes necessary.

With Roca, we have developed a dry tile application system. The pieces are screwed into place without the need for grout, and are avai-

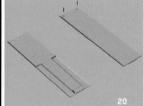
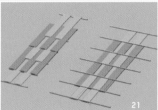
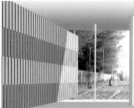

lable in a range of colours. Their large dimensions (30 x 120 cm) also facilitates fitting. The back of the tile is designed (**20**) such that the pieces can be placed in an overlapping shingle-like fashion (**21**).

In bathrooms this system facilitates removal of the tiles and thus refurbishment and access to plumbing and wiring, without producing rubble or noise. The elegant texture also makes the tiles appropriate for all spaces, especially those adjacent to patios, courtyards or gardens: wherever, due to weathering, the cladding material is subject to change, these porcelain stoneware tiles offer continuity and favour spatial fluidity between the interior and the exterior (**22**).

These concepts, from the simplest to the most utopian, are all part of a new joint effort by manufacturers and architects. Thus architects, instead of resigning themselves to working in isolation on their designs, form a new intercommunicative nexus with the tile manufacturing sector in order to generate new ideas and promote projects of mutual interest — which can only further strengthen an industry that is already a world leader.

VICENTE SARRABLO PhD in Architecture from the School of Architecture of Barcelona (ETSAB) at the Technical University of Catalonia (UPC).
Director of the Chair of Ceramic Studies, he is also Tutor and Director of the Construction Department at School of Architecture of the International University of Catalonia.
Specialist in technological innovation with ceramic materials, in fast-assembly industrialized construction and in advanced design of pneumatic structures. In these fields he has several works, distinctions, publications and research projects.

Spain: a meeting place and departure point for ceramics

In the Middle Ages the Iberian peninsula became a meeting place for different ceramic traditions in which factors as diverse as the decorative repertory of the Egypto- Mesopotamian tradition, the rich tradition in ceramics of the Romans and Visigoths, the strong influence of ceramics from the Islamic world and the Christian world with Central European and Mediterranean origins played a significant role. The result was an artistic panorama which, despite the disparity of the original essentials, achieved a surprising degree of coherence in its aesthetic aspects.

The first examples of glazed ceramics in architecture appeared towards the end of the 11th century in Almohad pavements and mural decorations found in Seville.

In Andalusia, in the 13th century, they used tiles called *a-zala iyi*, which had a wide range of tones and replaced the marble used previously in the Muslims tradition to decorate their houses. These pieces, with their perfection of geometric forms, illustrate the evolution of Hispano-Muslim design.

The location of the great centres of production, in Granada, Seville, Toledo, Manises-Paterna, Teruel and many other places, coincides with the most important Mudejar enclaves and also, more or less, with the future focal points of production of modern times.

There are whole periods of the history of architecture where it is impossible to describe the buildings without making a constant reference to ceramics. Spain has played the lead role in at least two of these periods: one of them began in the 13th century when work started on the Alhambra and was continued by later Andalusian architects; the other is the Art Nouveau period (end of 19th century, beginning of 20th century) which, although it was mainly centred in Catalonia, had a notable and widespread cultural impact and marked the production of ceramics, mainly manufactured in Castellón, during forty long years.

Spain is heir to a rich historical tradition. Today, it is one of the most important production centres in the world, at the forefront of the design, innovation and manufacture of ceramic tiles. Over 90% of production in Spain — i.e., 45% of European production — is concentrated in the province of Castellón, where manufacturers of ceramic claddings, secondary and service industries, ceramic design and R & D centres are congregated. And 55% of Spanish production is exported to 185 countries around the world.

ASCER, the Spanish Ceramic Tile Manufacturers Association, represents 99% of Spanish ceramics production. Based in the province of Caste-llón, it promotes the use of ceramic tiles and the knowledge of its advantages and applications, both in Spain and abroad, and stands as a fundamental point of reference for specifiers who wish to learn more about the industry and its products for architecture.

With this in view, ASCER offers the information services and carries out promotional activities such as:

Tile of Spain Awards of Architecture and Interior Design
This is an annual international event. It rewards the use of ceramics in the formal part of projects in the categories of architecture and interior design. Some award-winners are discussed in this book.

Chair of Ceramic Studies in collaboration with the School of Architec-ture of the International University of Catalonia to study and research the possibilities of ceramics in the field of architecture. (see page 152, article by Vicente Sarrablo)

"Tile of Spain" international promotional programme involves the follo-wing activities:
- Seminars and technical workshops on ceramics, for architects and designers. The seminars are a good opportunity to learn more about the technical characteristics and advantages of ceramics in construction. Special attention is paid to the United States, where architects may obtain Continuing Education Units' (C.E.U.) by attending the seminars.
- Information point at the headquarters of ASCER and the "Tile of Spain" promotional centres in Miami, London, Düsseldorf, Paris and Moscow. They provide information on ceramics produced in Spain as well as informative publications.
- Press relations office for architectural publications.
- Organisation of visits to Spain by delegations of international journalists for the presentation of novelties in ceramics and new architectural applications.
- Training programmes for recently graduated architects at the headquarters of ASCER and visits to ceramic tiles production centres.

Spain also hosts two of the main world events in the ceramics sector:

Qualicer, the prestigious world congress on ceramic tile quality, held in Castellón every two years, which is an indispensable reference point for technicians and other professionals from the world of ceramics.

Cevisama, the world ceramics exhibition held annually in Valencia.

Published by
ASCER
Spanish Ceramic Tile Manufacturers'
Association

Edited by
Armelle Tardiveau
in collaboration with
Vicente Sarrablo
Javier Soriano (ASCER)

Articles' texts
Toni Cumella i Vendrell
Rafael Diez Barreñada
Manuel González
Mila Payá
Javier Mira Peidro
Jordi Roviras Miñana
Cristina García Castelao
Fernando Ramos Galino
Anna Ramos Sanz
Vicente Sarrablo

Projects' texts
Their authors except for the Jenny
and Luc Peire Foundation: Marc Dubois

Transaltions and proof-reading
Christopher Gladwin
Ted Krasny

Graphic design
Manuel Cuyàs

Production
Actar Pro

Printing
Ingoprint SA

Photographs
Ángel Baltanás
Jordi Bernadó
Hélène Binet
Lluís Casals
Francesc Català-Roca
CRAFT
Toni Cumella
Max Dupain
Jean-Christophe Dupuy
Luís Ferreira Alves
Yukio Futagawa
Toni Gironès
Roland Halbe
Gary Kirkham
Peter Leeb
Duccio Malagamba
Yuzo Mikami
Satoru Mishima
Paul Ott
Ramon Prat
Christian Richters
Simo Rista
Eva Serrats
Rupert Steiner
Crombie Taylor
Crombie Träskelin

Distribution
Actar D
Roca i Batlle, 2
08023 Barcelona
Tel + 34 93 417 49 93
Fax + 34 93 418 67 07
office@actar-d.com
www.actar.es

ISBN 84-609-9212-8
DL B-5953-2006

Printed and bound in Spain